Published in Augusta, GA by Willis Family Media, LLC.
Willis Family Media titles may be purchased in bulk for
educational, business, fundraising or sales promotional use.
For information, please contact us.

Unless otherwise noted, Scriptures are taken from the Holy
Bible, ESV, NIV and NLT:

English Standard Version (ESV)
The Holy Bible, English Standard Version. ESV® Permanent
Text Edition® (2016). Copyright © 2001 by Crossway Bibles,
a publishing ministry of Good News Publishers.

New International Version (NIV)
Holy Bible, New International Version®, NIV® Copyright
©1973, 1978, 1984, 2011 by Biblica, Inc.® Used by permission.
All rights reserved worldwide.

New Living Translation (NLT)
Holy Bible, New Living Translation, copyright © 1996, 2004,
2015 by Tyndale House Foundation. Used by permission of
Tyndale House Publishers Inc., Carol Stream, Illinois 60188.
All rights reserved.

The Library of Congress Cataloging-in-Publication
Data is on file with the Library of Congress
ISBN: 978-0692800256 (Willis Family Media, LLC)

7 DAYS TO A

Stronger

Marriage

Husbands Edition

*Grow closer to your wife
than ever before.*

DAVE & ASHLEY WILLIS

CONTENTS

INTRODUCTION

Welcome to the 7 Days to a Stronger Marriage journey! Over the course of the next week, we believe that your marriage could become stronger than ever. We've spent years gathering marriage advice from couples from all over the world, we've studied the timeless truths that the Bible teaches about marriage, we've explored modern research on healthy relationship dynamics and we've combined it all together to create a one-week journey that can make an immediate impact in your marriage.

This book contains seven chapters that are meant to be read one chapter per day over the course of seven days. Each chapter takes one specific promise from the traditional marriage vows and explores its meaning and implications in detail. After the daily reading, there will be an activity assignment for you to do based on the reading and there is also a journaling section where you can record your thoughts, prayers and new ideas throughout the process. The final activity at the end of day seven will incorporate each of the vows and will give you a creative way to renew your vows to your wife.

There are also some rules we'll ask you to adopt over the course of the next week in addition to the readings and activities. These rules are designed to create a positive tone in your home and cultivate an environment where the full impact of the marriage challenge can be realized. The rules might also help you start some new healthy habits that can continue long after the week is over.

This experience is meant to be done in partnership with your wife. Hopefully she already has the wives edition of the book and she's excited to take this journey with you. While it's our hope that couples do this challenge with equal enthusiasm, we know that in some cases, a husband might be doing this challenge without the full partnership of his wife. If you are taking this challenge to invest into your marriage and you feel like you're in it alone, please don't lose hope! These readings and activities can make an impact in your marriage and a positive impression on your wife, even if she is not currently participating. Your efforts might eventually inspire her to take the challenge with you.

As you start this journey, know that you are pursuing something that is well worth the time and energy you're going to invest. Any investment into your marriage is always an investment worth making! We are praying for you and cheering you on in the days ahead. Please feel free to contact us to let us know how the experience is going and how we can encourage you.

Thanks and God bless,
Dave and Ashley Willis
www.AshleyWillis.org
www.DaveWillis.org

7 DAY MARRIAGE CHALLENGE

THE
RULES
FOR THE

THE RULES FOR THE
7 DAY MARRIAGE CHALLENGE

In addition to your daily readings and daily activities outlined on the pages ahead, there are some ground rules we are challenging you to implement. Adhering to these rules will cultivate an atmosphere where your marriage can be at its best over the course of the next seven days. We also challenge you to keep these habits long after the challenge has ended.

I _____ (your name) will wholeheartedly participate in the 7 Day Marriage Challenge over the next seven days as a way to renew my vows, recharge my marriage and recommit to my wife. I understand that the benefits I receive from this experience will be in direct correlation to the efforts I invest. I am committing to completing each of the daily readings and daily activities. In addition, I am adopting the following four commitments for the next seven days:

1.

I will say nothing negative to my wife or about my wife. I will not use negative words or a negative tone in my voice. I understand that the tone of my words will shape the tone of my marriage and I'm committing to make it positive. If I break this commitment, I will immediately apologize.

2.

I will make daily communication with my wife a priority. I will carve out at least thirty minutes of uninterrupted time for us to discuss the daily readings and complete the daily activity. In addition, I will strive to make myself available to her this week like never before. I will plan at least one date night without children. I'll call and/or text her throughout the day as much as our schedules allow. I'll show her the place of priority she has in my schedule and in my heart by being available to her.

3.

I will also prioritize the physical intimacy in our relationship by making time to make love at least three times over the course of the next seven days. I understand that it takes much more than sex to build a strong marriage, but it's nearly impossible to build a strong marriage without it. I will make it a priority.

4.

I will pray with and for my wife each day this week. I will pray with her (aloud) and thank God for specific reasons I feel thankful to have her in my life. I'll ask God for specific prayer requests I have for our marriage. I'll confess specific struggles and sins I need help to overcome and I'll ask my wives forgiveness for anything I've done to hurt her. Even if my wife is not willing to pray with me, I'm still committed to pray for her and for our marriage each day.

_____   2/10/2019
Signed   Date

A PRAYER FOR MY WIFE

Part of the rules for the challenge includes praying for your wife daily. This might be a new exercise for you, so to give you some words, we have included a sample prayer on the following page. Please feel free to use this as a template or just a starting point if you'd prefer to pray in your own words. I'm convinced that our prayers aren't about the actual words nearly as much as the heart behind them.

Lord, thank you for sending me such an incredible partner, best friend and wife. Next to your grace, her love is the greatest gift in my life. Please never let me take her for granted. Help me to love, cherish, respect, adore and protect her the way that she deserves. I know she's not only my wife, she's your daughter and you've trusted me to be her husband. Please help me to love her the way that you love her; being willing to lay down my life for her the way you have done for us.

Father, we live in a world where your daughters are being objectified and used as images for lust and selfish gratification. Please help me keep my eyes and my heart pure in a world of sin and exploitation. Help me have eyes only for my wife. Give her the confidence to know that she'll never have to compete for my attention against an airbrushed image of another woman. Let her know that I'm now and always captivated by her inner beauty and her outer beauty as well. Please keep her away from the comparison trap that would shatter her confidence and replace it with insecurity.

Help her know she doesn't need to compare her life or her accomplishments to anyone else's because your plan for her is masterfully unique. Help me to be her biggest encourager and never her biggest critic. Give me the words to say when she needs encouragement and give me the wisdom to know when to shut up and be quiet when she just needs me to listen.

Help me to support her dreams and passions to propel her to achieving all you have for her. For all she will achieve, please don't let her fall into the trap of believing her identity is wrapped up in achievements (or failures) but her identity is secured in your love for her. Never let her lose sight of the fact that she's eternally loved by you and let her find strength in my love for her as well.

Fill her heart with joy. Let laughter fill the soundtrack of our life together. Even in the difficult seasons, help us choose joy as we're reminded that our struggles are temporary but because of you Lord, our joy will be eternal. Help me be strong for her on the days she's feeling weak and help her be strong for me on the days I'm feeling weak, and Lord, please give us both strength for all that's ahead. Help us to never lose faith in you or give up on each other.

Thank you, Lord, for my amazing wife! She's a priceless gift to be treasured and I pray that you'd help me to be a gift to her as well. Please give me the wisdom, courage and strength to be the best husband I can be today and everyday. In Jesus' name, Amen.

DAY
ONE
_

I TAKE YOU TO BE MY WIFE

I remember it like it was yesterday. I had just returned home for summer break and I was starting work at a camp before heading back to college for my senior year. Ashley and I had been talking about marriage since our third date and the time had come to get the ring and plan a perfect evening to propose. I wanted to close the deal fast before she realized that she was way out of my league and could probably find a much better guy if she looked around!

With the help of her parents, I planned an elaborate story to give me an excuse to go and do some prep work. I told her that I needed to go visit my brother who had just broken his collarbone. I hadn't thought through my backstory very well because she said she wanted to come with me, so in a panic, I blurted out, "You can't...he's naked!"

"What? Why is he naked"

"I don't know. When he's injured, he likes to be naked. I know, it's weird, but you can't come. He wouldn't want you to see him like that."

She was disappointed and confused when I left. I had knots in my stomach from nervousness and from the guilt of just having told her a ridiculous lie. To this day, I'm terrible at lying to her, which has actually worked out to be great for our marriage!

I finally made it back to take her to dinner and everything was ready to go. She looked absolutely stunning in a red dress that brought out the beautiful tones of her strawberry blonde hair. I kept thinking, "No way is she going to say, 'yes.' She is way out of my league!"

We went out to the nicest restaurant in town and I paid a small fortune for a meal that I was too nervous to eat. We finally made it to the spot where I was going to pop the question. It was a placed called "Ashland" which is the estate of the famous Kentucky Statesman, Henry Clay. The weather and the scenery were beautiful.

My hands were shaking as I pulled out a handwritten letter and began reading it to her. I professed my undying love and commitment to her and I promised to always love and cherish her and to build our future on a foundation of faith in God. I got down on one knee and asked her to spend her life with me and she took a deep breath and exclaimed, "No way!"

My heart sank until I realized that it was a good "no way" and she hugged me and said, "Yes!" That began a journey that led us to a beautiful wedding day where we exchanged those timeless vows, beginning with the promise,

"I Dave, take you, Ashley, to be my wife."

"I Ashley, take you, Dave, to be my husband."

Our journey has been a beautiful one since the day we exchanged those vows, but we've come to discover that being a husband and being a wife is more complex than we first realized. We both had a desire to become a perfect spouse and we soon discovered that God's definition of a healthy marriage is often different than what we see in the world around us.

THE PERFECT HUSBAND:

MAN'S VIEW VS. GOD'S VIEW

We all have in our minds what a perfect spouse looks like and it is often a picture we get from the world's superficial value system rather than from God. The Bible says that people tend to look at the outward appearance, while God looks at the heart. He doesn't measure the worth of a husband or wife by how much money he might have in the bank or by how much she weighs. It's an issue of the heart and He has given us a clear path to follow.

For husbands, our role model is Jesus. You might be thinking, "Wait a minute, I didn't think Jesus was ever even married?" You are correct, He was never married. But Jesus is often referred to as the "bridegroom" and husbands are called to imitate the relationship Jesus has with His bride, which is the church. Based on the example of Jesus, here are a few key roles that every husband must strive to fill each and every day:

1. A HUSBAND LOVES HIS WIFE PASSIONATELY AND SELFLESSLY.

Jesus was the embodiment of love and He showed us that love is much more about action and commitment than it is about feeling. He pursued us passionately and then displayed the ultimate love by dying in our place on the cross. The Bible specifically calls husbands to love their wives with that same type of selfless love.

2. A HUSBAND SERVES HIS WIFE.

Jesus was a king, but He laid down His rights to be served and instead He served others. As husbands, we are called to serve our wives and families. In practical terms this means placing their needs ahead of our wants. It means prioritizing them ahead of our hobbies or even our careers. It means being willing to do dishes, fold laundry or whatever else is needed to support our families.

3. A HUSBAND PROTECTS HIS WIFE.

Jesus was described as a shepherd. In His culture, a shepherd was one who would protect the sheep from any form of attack-even if it meant risking his own life in the process. As husbands, we are called to be the protectors of our wives and children. God gave you those manly muscles for a reason! Physical protection is one part of the equation but we all need to be emotional and spiritual protectors as well. This means speaking words of encouragement and hope instead of belittling or demanding. It also means accepting God's call to lead our families into deeper spiritual maturity.

4. A HUSBAND PROVIDES FOR HIS WIFE.

Jesus provides every need-both great and small. He has set the example of the husband as provider by giving sight to a blind man, giving food to the hungry masses that hadn't eaten lunch, providing wine at a wedding banquet and even giving His own life to bring salvation. Providing financially is one part of this, but don't use that as an excuse to work so much that you are absent from your family. The greatest gift Jesus provided was giving Himself and the greatest gift you can provide is the gift of yourself. Part of providing means simply providing your own presence. Your wife and family can do with less of almost anything if it means having more of you.

5. A HUSBAND COMMUNICATES OPENLY AND HONESTLY WITH HIS WIFE.

Most frustrations in marriage come either directly or indirectly from a breakdown in communication between husband and wife. Men and women both contribute to the communication breakdown in different ways. For men, the breakdown often comes through a lack of communication. Our wives need for us to talk to them and not just the way we talk about the weather or football with our guy friends. They need us to share the details of your day and listen carefully to what they are trying to communicate to us. Speak with truth and love and listen with respect and compassion. If you'll make communication a priority, I believe every other aspect of your marriage will begin to improve.

THE PERFECT WIFE:

MAN'S VIEW VS. GOD'S VIEW

In our culture, a "trophy wife" is one whose husband wants to show her off as a symbol of status. She's typically portrayed as a much younger woman with a perfect figure, designer clothes and not a hair out of place. While there's definitely nothing wrong with beauty or fitness, God defines a good wife in terms of her character. The example of this "wife of noble character" is outlined in chapter thirty-one of the Bible's Book of Proverbs and her character traits are listed below. We're not listing these traits of wives as a way to give you a checklist to use to critique your wife. Rather, we put both lists in both editions of the book so that you can have some healthy perspective and dialogue about the different needs, desires and responsibilities both spouses possess.

1. A WIFE BRINGS RESPECT TO HER HUSBAND.

Notice that she doesn't just give respect, but she actually brings respect. Her words and actions towards her husband actually have the power to either build him up or tear him down. Proverbs paints a picture of a man being more respected and more respectable because of the honor his wife has brought to him.

2. A WIFE PROVIDES A SAFE HOME FOR HER HUSBAND.

A wife of noble character will make it her mission to have a home full of peace and joy. There will always be moments of chaos along the way because that's just how life works, but she strives to create a life-giving environment. The wife is the "heart of the home" and she is the person most capable of creating the mood and climate in the home; so she strives to create a good one!

3. A WIFE PROVIDES SEXUAL INTIMACY FOR HER HUSBAND.

The number one physical and emotional need for most men is sex. A wife should realize the power of sex and strive to make it a priority. An enriching sex life will ultimately enrich every other aspect of the marriage. It is a God-given gift meant to create a physical, emotional and spiritual bond between husband and wife. What happens in the bedroom has the power to set the tone for the entire marriage.

4. A WIFE LOOKS HER BEST FOR HER HUSBAND.

While outward appearance isn't everything, a wife must realize that God created men to be visual creatures and she honors her husband and her marriage when she strives to look her best.

5. A WIFE PROVIDES COMPANIONSHIP FOR HER HUSBAND.

One of the most important roles for a wife is simply to be a best friend to her husband. He desires your companionship. At the core of every healthy marriage is a healthy friendship.

BEING THE BEST HUSBAND YOU CAN BE

There is a temptation to read through the roles of the husband and the wife and instead of looking for ways that you need to improve, you only see the ways your wife needs to improve and do a better job of meeting your needs. It doesn't work that way! It is never your job to point out the flaws of your wife; it's only your job to be the best husband that you can be. You must take full responsibility for your role in the relationship and serve your wife even when you feel she doesn't deserve it.

You might need to ask yourself some difficult questions. Ask, "Was I a better husband at the beginning of our relationship than I am right now? Have I stopped giving the best of myself to my marriage? Am I treating my wife the way I want to be treated?"

Don't slip into the common trap of what we call a "cable company marriage." Ashley and I were reminded of one of the most common mistakes in marriage recently when a salesman appeared at our front door to pitch a new cable TV company. He promised the best rates and channels and it was all guaranteed for the first year. He was giving us everything he had to offer and asking for very little in return. We asked what happened after the first year and he sheepishly said, "Well, you only get the best at the beginning. After a year, the cost goes up and the service goes down. That's how everyone does it." Cable companies seem to treat their customers amazingly when they're first trying to seal the deal. Once they've got you, the introductory rates disappear and are replaced with much more expensive rates. In addition, the customer service takes a nose dive, which makes you want to trade in your old cable company for a new one. The cable TV industry seems focused on a model of treating people really well at first, then taking them for granted in the long run.

Sadly, a lot of marriages operate this way too. In the beginning, when a couple is trying to win each other's hearts, they roll out the red carpet. They give the very best of themselves but it doesn't last long. Once the day-to-day reality of life sets in, they stop doing all those things they did in the beginning. They take each other for granted and it isn't long before they both start longing to leave for something new where they'll be treated well again. Don't settle for a "cable company marriage!" Don't give the best of yourselves at the beginning, but then give less and less as time goes on.

Don't take each other for granted. Any marriage left on autopilot will eventually crash. One of the best ways to keep your marriage from slipping into this common trap is to ask each other, "What are some habits we had at the beginning of our relationship that we've stopped and we need to start again?" And, "What are some habits that we've formed that we need to get rid of for the sake of our marriage?"

BUILDING YOUR MARRIAGE ON THE RIGHT FOUND-ATION

As Christians, we wholeheartedly believe the Bible's truths have practical application to every part of life. Even if you don't share our faith, we believe these timeless truths from the Bible can revolutionize your marriage. These wise teachings have built the foundation for our own marriage and Bible teachings continue to shape our own understandings about life, love and marriage. We challenge you to give them a try! They've been working for thousands of years and these principles will work for your marriage too.

10 Foundational Principles about Marriage
in the Bible (in no particular order):

1. SEX SHOULD BE A PRIORITY FOR BOTH SPOUSES.

Since God invented sex (THANKS, God), He has a lot to say about how it should be used and enjoyed. It's meant to be used often in marriage with both spouses submitting to each other's needs and desires. Making love should be a high priority in your marriage. Seriously. Frequency and intimacy in the bedroom will bring greater intimacy to all other aspects of the marriage as well.

"The husband should fulfill his wife's sexual needs, and the wife should fulfill her husband's needs. The wife gives authority over her body to her husband, and the husband gives authority over his body to his wife." *1 Corinthians 7:3-4*

2. JESUS TAUGHT THAT LUST IS ACTUALLY A FORM OF ADULTERY.

We tend to believe as long as we don't commit a sex act with someone outside the marriage, then we're being monogamous. God's standard for monogamy includes not only what happens in the bedroom, but what happens in the mind. This includes pornography, graphic romance novels, checking out other people, etc. It's a high standard but it's because marriage is a high priority.

"You have heard the commandment that says, "You must not commit adultery.' But I say, anyone who even looks at a woman with lust has already committed adultery with her in his heart." *Matthew 5:27-28*

3. LOVE IS AN UNCONDITIONAL COMMITMENT, NOT A FICKLE FEELING.

Couples who talk about falling out of love don't really have a grasp of what love actually means. Love, by its very nature, isn't a fairy tale feeling, but a commitment. Love is a choice much more than feeling. It's rooted in commitment much more than compatibility. Love isn't a story with a happy ending; love is a story with no ending.

"Love never gives up, never loses faith, is always hopeful, and endures through every circumstance." *1 Corinthians 13:7*

4. EVERY WIFE NEEDS LOVE AND EVERY HUSBAND NEEDS RESPECT.

Both men and women need love and respect, but men tend to have a unique desire for respect and appreciation while women have a unique desire for love and adoration.

One of the toughest parts of marriage is giving love when your spouse is acting unlovable or giving respect when they're acting disrespectful. God gives us His best when we're at our worst and He calls us to do that for each other in marriage. People usually need love most when they deserve love least.

"So again I say, each man must love his wife as he loves himself and the wife must respect her husband." *Ephesians 5:33*

5. GOD HATES DIVORCE (BUT HE LOVES DIVORCED PEOPLE).

God is full of love and the Bible doesn't give many examples of things God hates, but divorce is on the list. God has so much love for marriage, his heart breaks over the pain of divorce (and our hearts should break too). There are certainly circumstances where divorce may be the only remaining option. Unfortunately, too many couples see divorce as a first response instead of a last resort.

"For I hate divorce!" says the Lord, the God of Israel. "To divorce your wife is to overwhelm her with cruelty," says the Lord of Heaven's Armies. "So guard your heart; do not be unfaithful to your wife." *Malachi 2:16*

If you are reading this and in a second marriage, please don't feel judged or shamed. When we read everything the Bible has to say about grace and the examples of all the great leaders in the Bible who fell short of God's standard, we're comforted in knowing God gives second chances and new beginnings. You can't change the past, but you can start now and build a new future with your new spouse.

6. YOUR SPOUSE'S NEEDS HAVE TO COME BEFORE YOUR OWN.

In our selfish human nature, we tend to look at every relationship (including marriage) as a way to get our own needs met, but marriage means laying down your own rights for the sake of another. This requires mutual submission and serving your spouse even when they're not reciprocating. This is modeled by how Jesus served us and even died for us when we were undeserving.

"And further, submit to one another out of reverence for Christ. For wives, this means submit to your husbands as to the Lord. For a husband is the head of his wife as Christ is the head of the church. He is the Savior of his body, the church. As the church submits to Christ, so you wives should submit to your husbands in everything. For husbands, this means love your wives, just as Christ loved the church. He gave up his life for her." *Ephesians 5:21-25*

7. A HUSBAND AND WIFE ARE UNITED IN EVERYTHING.

There can't be "his" and "hers" when it comes to money, hopes, dreams or struggles. Marriage means sharing everything. It means keeping no secrets from each other. This means your disagreements won't have a "winner" and a "loser" because you'll either win together or lose together every time. It means remembering that you should never let your spouse walk alone because you're unified in everything.

"This explains why a man leaves his father and mother and is joined to his wife and the two are united into one." *Genesis 2:24*

8. A MARRIAGE TAKES THREE.

We are not talking about polygamy here (although some in the Bible practiced it and caused a lot of family drama as a result). The third member of a marriage is God Himself. He created marriage not just to be a man and a woman, but rather, a man and a woman in a growing relationship with each other and with God. The more you love God, the more capacity you will have to love each other.

"God is love. Whoever lives in love lives in God, and God in them." *1 John 4:16*

9. A HUSBAND AND WIFE SHOULD NEVER KEEP SECRETS FROM EACH OTHER.

The very first picture of marriage we see in the Bible was illustrated by nakedness. This obviously gives us a vivid picture of the importance of physical nakedness in marriage. Nakedness in the Bible also represents and emotional vulnerability and transparency. The strongest marriages are "naked marriages" which means there are no secrets, hidden passwords, hidden purchases, hidden money or anything else. The level of your transparency will determine the level of your trust and the stronger your trust, the stronger your marriage will be.

"Adam and his wife were both naked, and they felt no shame." *Genesis 2:25*

10. YOUR FIRST LOYALTY SHOULD ALWAYS BE TO YOUR SPOUSE.

The Bible talks about "leaving and cleaving." It's a clear call to loyalty. Once we're married, we can no longer place other family members or other pursuits ahead of the marriage. Your spouse has to come first. Defend each other. Protect each other. Be there for each other.

"That is why a man leaves his father and mother and is united to his wife, and they become one flesh." *Genesis 2:24*

Work together to apply these Biblical principles into your marriage and we believe you'll be amazed at the results.

HOW TO HAVE A HAPPY WIFE

I want to end this first chapter with a man-to-man discussion about how to have a happy wife. I'm inviting you into the conversation my Dad had with me years ago, which contained some of the best marriage advice I've ever received. This simple lesson changed my marriage for the better and it can change your marriage too! When I was engaged and just a few days away from the wedding, my wise Dad said, "Son, always invest the best of yourself into your marriage. Put your wife ahead of yourself. Strive to make her a happy woman. A happy wife creates a happy life."

My parents have a wonderful marriage. They're best friends. They love each other and they actually like each other too! They have the kind of marriage that made me genuinely excited about getting married someday, so I took dad's advice to heart. I've found it to be completely true! When Ashley is happy, I'm happy.

Now, you might be asking, "How can I make my wife happy?" That's a great question and a complicated one because I don't think it's possible for one person to make another person happy. In fact, when we expect a spouse to make us happy, both spouses usually end up unhappy. A lot of marriages struggle because both spouses are unhappy and blame each other for their unhappiness. Still, I've learned that there are some very specific ways a husband can and should cultivate happiness and joy for his wife. Many places in this book will contain lists of things to do but I'm going to do something different here. I'm going to share just one thing because I'm convinced that if you'll do this one thing, it will create more happiness for your wife and more peace and joy in your marriage. I've found we all tend to learn best through stories, so I'm going to illustrate this one principle through a true story that just happened in our marriage.

Ashley and I recently had the opportunity to take on a project that would instantly bring a good amount of additional income. I wanted to do it! I was already mentally spending the extra money. The problem is that the stress and strain of this project was going to fall mostly on Ashley. She's already working so hard in so many areas and she doesn't have much extra margin to take on new projects. She saw that I was excited about the opportunity, so to be supportive and encouraging to me, she agreed to do it. She's always so willing to support me (even when my ideas are bad)! As we started making preparations to begin the project, I sensed the stress she was feeling. She insisted that she was fine and willing to take on the extra workload, but I knew she didn't have peace about it. I made the decision to pull the plug. I knew that no amount of extra money would be worth taking joy or peace away from her. I told her that I didn't want to do it because I'd much rather have the extra peace and joy in our home than the extra money and stress. I could see the weight of that stress lift off her shoulders and then she gave me that smile that still melts my heart every time! Honestly, it was a no-brainer. That little bit of extra money wouldn't have meant much when I'm at the end of my life looking back. I thought to myself, there's no price tag I could ever place on my relationship with Ashley. Giving up this money was a small (but also a tangible) way that I could show her the place of priority she will always have in my heart.

So, what's that one thing a husband should do to make his wife happy? It goes back to what my dad said to me all those years ago. It's simply to prioritize your wife's needs ahead of your own agenda. It's to show her that you value your marriage more than your money. It's showing her that her happiness is the key to your own happiness. It's showing her that she matters to you more than anything or anyone else.

I can't make my wife happy but I've learned that I can fuel Ashley's happiness when she knows that I value her above any other relationship, pursuit or agenda. When she knows that she doesn't have to compete with my career, my hobbies or anything else to have the best of my time and attention, it gives her confidence and joy. When she knows that I'm willing to sacrifice my own agenda for the good of our marriage, she feels protected and cherished. She deserves my best; not my leftovers. When I'm willing to give my best, she's much happier and so am I.

I fail at this often, but when I remember this lesson and apply it to my marriage, it makes a huge difference. Over the next seven days (and beyond) please be intentional about giving your wife your very best; not your leftovers. You'll be amazed at the difference it will make in her happiness (and yours too).

KEEPING THE FIRST PROMISE:

"I TAKE YOU TO BE MY WIFE."

As you live out this first promise, remember that your vow means you are choosing each and every day to honor your wife over anyone else. You are waking each morning with a renewed commitment to be her best and most loyal friend. You are agreeing to fulfill your unique, God-given roles as a husband to the very best of your abilities and you are acknowledging that it is never your responsibility to point out all the ways that your wife is falling short. Support her, pray for her and encourage her so that you both may become the best spouse that you can be.

DAY

ONE

Activity

Ashley and I have spent years collecting great nuggets of marriage advice and we've compiled our "Top 25" into this list below. Read through this list with your wife and one at a time discuss how you feel you are currently doing at applying each one of these in your marriage. Give each one a score of "always," "sometimes" or "never." Then pick three from this list that you'd like to start prioritizing in your marriage. It could lead to some great conversations!

1. Choose to love each other even in those moments when you struggle to like each other. Love is a commitment, not a feeling.

Sometimes

2. Always answer the phone when your husband/wife is calling and when possible, try to keep your phone off when you're together with your spouse.

Sometimes

3. Make time together a priority. Budget for a consistent date night. Time is the "currency of relationships," so consistently invest time into your marriage.

Sometimes

4. Surround yourself with friends who will strengthen your marriage and remove yourself from people who may tempt you to compromise your character.

Sometimes

5. Make laughter the soundtrack of your marriage. Share moments of joy, even in the hard times find reasons to laugh.

Sometimes

6. In every argument, remember that there won't be a "winner" and a "loser." You are partners in everything so you'll either win together or lose together. Work together to find a solution.

Never

7. Remember that a strong marriage rarely has two strong people at the same time. It's usually a husband and wife taking turns being strong for each other in the moments when the other feels weak. (This is one of the many wise nuggets from my amazing wife Ashley!)

Sometimes

8. Prioritize what happens in the bedroom. It takes more than sex to build a strong marriage, but it's nearly impossible to build a strong marriage without it!

Sometimes

9. Remember that marriage isn't 50-50, divorce is 50-50. Marriage has to be 100-100. It's not splitting everything in half, but both partners giving everything they've got!

Sometimes

10. Give your best to each other, not your leftovers after you've given your best to everyone else.

Sometimes

11. Learn from other people, but don't feel the need to compare your life or your marriage to anyone else's. God's plan for your life is masterfully unique! *Never*

12. Don't put your marriage on hold while you're raising your kids or else you'll end up with an empty nest and an empty marriage.

Sometimes

13. Never keep secrets from each other. Secrecy is the enemy of intimacy. *Sometimes*

14. Never lie to each other. Lies break trust and trust is the foundation of a strong marriage.

Sometimes

15. When you've made a mistake, admit it and humbly seek forgiveness. You should be quick to say, "I was wrong. I'm sorry. Please forgive me."

Sometimes

16. When your husband/wife breaks your trust, give them your forgiveness instantly which will promote healing and create the opportunity for trust to be rebuilt. You should be quick to say, "I love you. I forgive you. Let's move forward."

Always

17. Be patient with each other. Your spouse is always more important that your schedule.

Sometimes

18. Model the kind of marriage that will make your sons want to grow up to be good husbands and your daughters want to grow up to be good wives.

Never

19. Be your spouse's biggest encourager, not his/her biggest critic. Be the one who wipes away their tears, not the one who causes them.

Sometimes

20. Never talk badly about your spouse to other people or vent about them online. Protect your spouse at all times and in all places.

~~Always~~ *Sometimes*

21. Always wear your wedding ring. It will remind you that you're always connected to your spouse and it will remind the rest of the world that you're off limits!

Always

22. Connect into a community of faith. A good church can make a world of difference in your marriage and family.

Sometimes

23. Pray together. Every marriage is stronger with God in the middle of it.

Sometimes

24. When you have to choose between saying nothing or saying something mean to your spouse, say nothing every time!

Sometimes

25. Never consider divorce as an option. Remember that a perfect marriage is just two imperfect people who refuse to give up on each other!

Sometimes

What did I learn about my spouse today?

What did I learn about my myself today?

As a result of what I'm learning, I'm committing to take the following actions to strengthen my marriage-

_____

_____

_____

_____

_____

_____

_____

_____

_____

_____

_____

_____

_____

_____

_____

_____

_____

Today, my prayer for my marriage is-

_____

_____

_____

_____

_____

_____

_____

_____

_____

_____

_____

_____

_____

_____

_____

_____

_____

DAY TWO

TO LOVE
AND TO
CHERISH

I have a good friend who lost his marriage because his wife didn't feel loved and cherished. For years, my friend worshipped his cars. He was a car nut. He knew everything about cars and would spend long hours honing the engine, waxing the paint and painstakingly caring for every detail of his prized possessions. He was good at it. So good, in fact, that he would spend his weekends at car shows where he accumulated a massive amount of trophies to confirm that his time on his vehicles had been well spent. The more trophies he won, the more he was motivated to work harder on his cars to win more trophies. All the while, his wife was miserable, but my friend was too busy to notice. When his wife was ready to leave him, in a moment of despair and absolute clarity, my friend looked at those trophies and he realized what they were...junk. They were idols that he had been worshipping instead of worshipping God. They were tangible evidence of thousands of hours he robbed from his wife and family and given to his hobby. They were an ugly reminder that he had loved and cherished things that couldn't love him back. He boxed up over one hundred trophies representing his blood, sweat and tears and he hauled them to a dumpster and threw them in the trash. He made a promise to God that he would never again put his work, his trophies, his money or anything else ahead of God and his family. His priorities would now and forever be:

1. His Faith

2. His Family

3. Everything and everyone else

What does your money and your time say about your priorities? The Bible says, "Where your treasure is, there your heart will be also." *Matthew 6:21* As men, we can be career-driven and tempted to pursue things with tangible rewards like money, promotions and trophies. The problem is that those things can't love us back. Your wife deserves your pursuit. She needs your love and adoration. If you want your marriage to thrive, you must be willing to put her above all those other things. What trophies do you need to throw away to remind your wife and yourself what matters most? Your spouse and your kids should always know that there is no trophy on earth that you value more than you value them. Let their pictures be what fills your trophy case. Let your love for them and your faith in God be what drives your ambition.

You'll never go astray when your priorities are in the right place.

Your marriage is a priceless trophy so spend your life investing into it. Give your wife your best; not your leftovers. Treasure your wife, spend time with your kids and build a legacy of love, laughter and faith in your family that will touch the world for generations to come! It all begins with a daily commitment to love and to cherish your wife.

WHAT
IS
LOVE?

This chapter (and really, all of marriage) is about love, but there are many different definitions of "love" in our world. Love is the foundation of a marriage, but to apply it properly, we need to begin with an understanding of what love really is. With so many definitions floating around, we'd like to bring it back to the source. God created love, so He is the only one qualified to define it.

The Bible has a lot to say about the subject of love. In fact, I believe love is the main point! There are many scriptures I could share to help us get a Biblical context of love and its meaning, but I'll focus in on "The Love Chapter" from 1 Corinthians 13. In this timeless passage, the Apostle Paul beautifully and poetically captures the essence of real love. This passage is widely considered to contain the most famous words about love ever written:

"Love is patient, love is kind. It does not envy, it does not boast, it is not proud. It does not dishonor others, it is not self-seeking, it is not easily angered, it keeps no record of wrongs. Love does not delight in evil but rejoices with the truth. It always protects, always trusts, always hopes, always perseveres. Love never fails." *1 Corinthians 13:4-7*

These famous words from Scripture aren't just a poetic description of love; they also represent a very practical roadmap to guide your marriage in the right direction. Make a conscious decision to love each other using God's definition of love as described in the Bible verse above. Allow your marriage to be led by love and you'll always be headed in the right direction!

Let's briefly unpack these verses about love and their practical application in your marriage. Love is patient and kind, so be patient and kind with each other. Love is not boastful or proud, so refuse to allow the poison of pride to taint your marriage. Love is not self-seeking, so choose to put your spouse's needs ahead of your own. Love is not easily angered, so allow no place for spite or hostility in your relationship. Love keeps no record of wrongs, so allow grace and forgiveness to flow freely. Love rejoices with the truth, so refuse to deceive or keep secrets from each other. Love always protects and perseveres, so never give up on each other!

Love is not enough to make a marriage work. We know that sounds very unromantic in a book about love and marriage, but love will never be enough to make a marriage work. The world defines love as a feeling and something we fall in and out of, which means we can lose the love that someone has already given us. This is especially disheartening when it comes to marriage. If love is just a fickle feeling, than how in the world can any of us stay married for life? The truth is, we can't if that's all there is to love.

Love (the way the Bible describes it) is rooted in unending commitment, healing, self-sacrifice and grace. That's real love. That's the kind of love that we want to have for our marriage—not some wishy-washy tepid love. We want the kind of love that lasts forever and we'd be willing to bet that's the kind of love you want for your marriage too.

Real love is always rooted in rock-solid commitment. When we are committed to someone or something, we offer that person or thing lots of time, attention and devotion. Sadly, there are many of us who are more committed to our hobbies and jobs than we are to our own families.

When we marry, we commit to love our spouse for all the days of our lives. When we have kids, we are committed to raising our kids to the best of our ability and to never give up on them, no matter what. In friendships, we are committed to being there for our friends in times of need and protecting their reputations. As Christians, we show our love and commitment to Christ by praying, reading the Word and doing what He's called us to do to the best of our ability.

LOVING YOUR WIFE REQUIRES KNOWING YOUR WIFE

_____

One of the greatest challenges in marriage is navigating the differences between the typical male thought process and the typical female thought process. God (in His wisdom and His sense of humor) gave men and women very different perspectives. When these differences are understood, the husband and wife can harmonize with each other and see the world with more depth and perspective than either can could do alone.

To help you understand the mind of your man, Ashley has listed below the main things that seem to dominate women's thoughts. I hope these insights spark some rich conversations in your marriage and this helps you understand your wife on a deeper level. I wrote a similar list about men in the "Wives Edition" of this book, so you and her can compare notes and hopefully have some great conversations!

The more that you and your wife can know and understand each other, the more you'll be able to express love to each other. If your wife is like most women, her thoughts are probably dominated by these ten questions that she asks herself almost every day (in no particular order):

1. WHAT IS ON THE TO-DO LIST TODAY (AND CAN I DO IT ALL)?

As women, we wear a lot of hats. Many of us have husbands, kids, jobs, homes, errands to run and the list goes on. We could spend a whole day taking care of each of these but we have to prioritize. So, most days, women are trying to do just that...take care of our loved ones and the many duties that come along with them. Oops, I forgot to put ourselves on the list, but this is often how it goes.

2. WOULD HE STILL CHOOSE ME?

This thought has nothing to do with confidence or even how we look. It has everything to do with the relationship we have with our husbands. We want to know that he still thinks we are "smokin' hot", as my husband says. We want to know that he only has eyes for us. Women long to be adored and prized, whether we are ill, pregnant, a little heavy or too thin. As wives, we are willing to do things to make ourselves attractive to our spouses and we want them to notice! Husbands, we see the way you look at us and we hear your words loud and clear. We want to know that you find us desirable on all levels; sexually (you love our body), mentally (you love our thoughts) and emotionally (you love our hearts). Let us know that you love being with us.

3. AM I SUCCEEDING AT MY JOB?

Just like men, women want to do the best job we can. We work hard and we want our hard work to pay off.

4. DO I HAVE MY PRIORITIES IN LINE?

As I mentioned before, women wear many hats and it is very difficult to juggle our many duties. As a wife and mother, I have felt "mommy guilt" when it comes to balancing duties at work and home. We want to be the best wife and mother possible while also having a successful career, if we are working outside of the home. It's a daily struggle to be carefully handled with lots of prayer.

5. AM I A GOOD WIFE?

Marriage is a blessing and we want to get it right. Sometimes our husbands can get placed on the back burner and then we start to see our relationship suffer. Husbands, we want to know that we are meeting your needs on all levels as much as we can. Many times, we are more willing to share our needs with our husbands more than they are willing to share their needs with us. We aren't mind readers! The more honest we can be with each other, the better. So, husbands, let us know, so we can be the best wives possible!

6. AM I A GOOD MOTHER?

In my current stage of life, I think I might word this question more like, "Am I messing up my kids?" Parenting is hard! It's honestly the hardest thing I have done thus far and I don't take it lightly. When we receive the blessing of motherhood, we immediately receive the weight that comes with it. We have visions of horror in thinking that thirty years down the road our grown children will have major issues and find us to blame. If only I had made him his favorite breakfast every morning, he would have felt more loved! If only I had been a little harder on him and had him do more chores, he wouldn't be so lazy! The struggle is real and messy, folks. Again, we just want to get it right.

7. AM I ENOUGH?

Sometimes, I don't feel like there is enough of me to go around and it can be exhausting. When I was teaching, I would wake up and pour into my husband and kiddos and spend some time in prayer. Once I arrived at school, I would pour into my students. Once I got back home, I would make dinner for my family, run my kids to their various activities and end the day by pouring into my husband and kids once again. I was honestly a shell of a person. I had been pouring out all day into the ones I love and doing something I loved to do, but I was completely spent. I would often lie in bed and think to myself, "Am I enough?" I think many women find themselves in the same boat. We often do so much but have so little to show for it at the time. We just want to know that we are enough.

8. AM I RESPECTABLE?

It has often been said that men desire respect and women want to be loved. I think this is true on many levels, but I think that women have a strong desire for respect as well. We want to know that our husbands, kids, friends and coworkers respect us. We don't like to be disrespected just like anyone else.

9. WHEN CAN I GET A BREAK?

Sometimes we just want a break. It could be a date night with our hubby, a girls night out with our friends or just a lazy, quiet night watching our favorite television shows while eating a big scoop of ice cream (or drinking a glass of wine, or hey, let's be real...both). For some reason, we feel guilty about needing this time, but everyone needs time to chill. Taking a couple of hours a week to reconnect with our husband, our friends or even ourselves is needed to lead a balanced life.

10. AM I MAKING A DIFFERENCE?

As a Christian, I think this might be the most important question I can ask myself. No matter where you might be in your faith, I truly believe that God designed each and every one of us with a significant purpose on Earth. Whether big or small, each of us has something good to offer the world. As women, we want to know that all the time and effort we put into our family, friendships, churches, charities/ministries and work is achieving a greater purpose and making the world a better place.

Ask your wife if this list is true for her. It might spark some wonderful conversations and help you learn more about each other in the process.

TRUE LOVE REQUIRES TRUE COMMITMENT

When life is hard and marriage seems to be more difficult than usual, our feelings will change. But our commitment can be unwavering when we choose to stay committed through thick and thin. That is precisely why love—as the world knows it and defines it—is not enough. But love—as God designed it and defines it—IS. We can't choose our feelings. We're human. But, you can choose to love someone enough to be committed to your wife. This is how marriage is supposed to work. When both partners choose to love each other by staying fully committed to one another on a daily basis, the marriage will thrive. Let's strive for that kind of love, friends; a love and a commitment that will never fail.

KEEPING THE SECOND PROMISE:

"I WILL LOVE & CHERISH YOU"

Love does for a marriage what breathing does for lungs, so do everything in your power to keep the love alive! Make time together a priority. Invest into your friendship with one another. Seek new ways to serve each other's needs. Through your words and your actions, consistently communicate your love, adoration and commitment to one another!

DAY
TWO

Activity

Before we get to today's activity, we're going to give you a sneak preview of the Day 7 activity because you might need several days to be working on it. Today's reading is all about loving and cherishing your wife. The final activity is going to be to read a "love letter" to her where you share some of the attributes you love about her. Write down words that you've perhaps never said aloud to her. You might be amazed by how much this letter will mean to her and if she's participating in the challenge with you, she'll have a love letter for you as well. These letters might become treasures for you both, so give plenty of time in planning and writing it.

Like yesterday's activity, today's activity will focus on growing closer to your wife through conversation and communication. There are twenty-one questions below designed to spark some new conversations. So often in marriage we get into a communication rut by having the same conversations about the same things over and over. These questions are designed to bring you two out of that rut and to infuse your communication with fresh perspective, laughter and fun. Carve out some time to ask each other these questions:

1. If there was a movie about your life, what songs would you want on the soundtrack?

2. In that movie, what actress (past or present) would you want to play you?

3. If you could have named yourself, what name would you have chosen?

4. What is your favorite thing about yourself?

5. What is one thing you wish you could change about yourself?

6. What was your biggest fear when you were a child?

7. What is your biggest fear now?

8. Besides our wedding and the day kids were born, what is your all-time favorite day?

9. What would you do with the money if we won the lottery?

10. What would you do tomorrow if you lost your job and money and we had to start over?

11. When you were a kid, who was your biggest hero?

12. Who is your biggest hero today?

13. What is your greatest regret?

14. What is one thing you'd like to accomplish by this time next year?

15. If you won a free vacation to any place on earth, where would you want to go?

16. What was your first nickname?

17. What is your earliest childhood memory?

18. What was the moment when you laughed harder than you've ever laughed?

19. If you could write one new law that everyone had to obey, what law would you create?

20. What's a new hobby you'd like to try out?

21. Besides marrying me...what's the greatest thing that has ever happened to you?

What did I learn about my spouse today?

_____

_____

_____

_____

_____

_____

_____

_____

_____

_____

_____

_____

_____

_____

_____

_____

_____

_____

_____

What did I learn about my myself today?

_____

_____

_____

_____

_____

_____

_____

_____

_____

_____

_____

_____

_____

_____

_____

_____

_____

_____

As a result of what I'm learning, I'm committing to take the following actions to strengthen my marriage-

_____

_____

_____

_____

_____

_____

_____

_____

_____

_____

_____

_____

_____

_____

_____

_____

_____

Today, my prayer for my marriage is-

_____

_____

_____

_____

_____

_____

_____

_____

_____

_____

_____

_____

_____

_____

_____

_____

_____

_____

_____

DAY THREE

"FOR BETTER OR FOR WORSE"

What's the hardest challenge in your marriage? Think about that question for a minute. Your answer says a lot about the current state of your relationship. For Ashley and I, the answer to that question has changed through the different seasons of our marriage. At one point it was financial stress. At another point it was managing complex family dynamics. At different points in marriage, we've wrestled with cross-country moves, depression, debt, parenting stress, work stress, health issues and many other challenges along the way. We've come to realize that struggles are always a part of marriage because struggles are always a part of life. It's how you choose to face those struggles that have a tremendous impact on the health of your marriage.

We had a conversation with a man at church recently that had been been married for fifty years. His words profoundly changed our perspective on struggles in marriage. He and his wife have walked through many struggles and many seasons of life in their half-century together. Their current struggles include a move from their hometown to be closer to family and a diagnosis of early Alzheimer's in his wife. Watching her battle dementia and lose her memories has clearly been one of the greatest struggles in their marriage, but apparently not his biggest struggle currently. His wife was on a weekend trip with their daughter spending some girl time together. We asked him how he's been doing and he said, "Honestly, I'm not doing so well." We didn't say it aloud, but we thought to ourselves, "Of course you're not! You are in a new town trying to learn a new routine and you are having to watch your wife slowly lose her memories and her personality through the cruel disease of Alzheimer's. Nobody in your shoes would be doing well."

What he said next left us speechless. When he was talking about why he was having such a hard time, his struggles had nothing to do with the factors we thought he meant. He said, "I'm having such a hard time because I love having her here with me. It has been years since I've had to go two days in a row without seeing her. I can't wait until she gets home tomorrow!" While so many couples seem to try and invent ways to escape from each other, this man and his wife and created a relationship that neither spouse ever wanted to escape. In fact, even the thought of being apart left him feeling sick. This temporary distance, not the Alzheimer's or anything else, was his current greatest struggle in marriage.

His perspective was an inspiring reminder to me that a marriage isn't defined by the size of your struggles but by the size of your commitment to overcome those struggles together. He felt he could face anything with his bride by his side and their united faith in God and faith in each other. No matter what life throws your way, your marriage will be able to survive any storm if you face it hand-in-hand and side-by-side with your spouse.

WHEN TRAGEDY STRIKES

———

Jay and Mandra are the kind of friends that anyone would love to have. To know them is to love them. When my family moved back to town a few years ago, Jay was the first one to show up to help us move in. He was also the last one to leave after single-handedly hauling most of our heaviest stuff. Moving heavy furniture definitely shows you who your friends are! One day out of the blue, a tragedy struck this amazing couple that would rock them to their very core. It was one of the worst phone calls I had ever received. I was at flag football practice with my six-year-old son when my cell phone rang. On the other end was the trembling voice of a police officer calling to inform me of what had just transpired.

Jay had been at home watching their three beautiful children while Mandra was out running some errands. Jay went inside with their baby to change a diaper while their four-year-old daughter, Jayden, continued to play in the backyard. Jay came back outside a few minutes later, but he didn't see Jayden. He began to walk around the yard calling out her name, but there was no response. He went back into the house and began calling out for her, but there was still no answer.

At this point, he started to panic, so he ran out into the street looking for her and checking with the neighbors. Nobody had seen her. In a moment of gut-wrenching terror, he realized that he had not checked the swimming pool. He hadn't considered it sooner because she was always so careful to stay away from it, but maybe there had been an accident and she had fallen in. He sprinted towards the pool and when he got there, he saw his daughter lying at the bottom. He instinctively dove in and pulled her out to begin CPR. In desperation, he scooped her up in his arms and ran to the nurse's house next door. She continued CPR until the ambulance arrived.

The next several hours were a blur. I arrived at the hospital shortly after receiving that phone call and I sat down with them in a private waiting room. The three of us cried, prayed and waited. We hoped for the best while trying to brace ourselves for the worst.

The doctor finally came in with a hospital chaplain beside him to deliver the news that we were praying not to hear. Their beautiful little girl was being kept alive by machines and there was nothing more that they could do for her. A few hours later, with her mother lying right beside her in the hospital bed, Jayden was pronounced dead. It was the darkest hour a husband and wife could possibly face.

Through the tears and pain, they held onto their faith in God and their faith in each other. As Jay was reliving the scene in his mind and beating himself up for not preventing it, Mandra was calmly rubbing his back and saying, "It's not your fault. You are an amazing father. You did everything you could have done. I love you so much."

That became a defining moment in their marriage. Many couples allow grief and tragedy to place a wedge between them, but Jay and Mandra chose to walk through their grief hand-in-hand and side-by-side. They knew that God was with them and that they would see their precious daughter again in Heaven. In the meantime, they were resolved to lean on each other and trust in God's goodness even when they couldn't make sense of the pain and loss they were experiencing.

Today, more than a year has passed since balloons were released and "Somewhere over the Rainbow" was sung in a touching celebration of Jayden's life at her preschool. Through their pain, Jay and Mandra continue to grow in their love for each other and for their beautiful children, Chloe and Austin. Jayden's legacy lives on in their hearts and in the many lives she touched in her four short years on earth. This family continues to inspire all who know them.

WHEN LIFE IS HARD

—

Most of us have never experienced tragedy like the one Jay and Mandra experienced and I pray you never will! Even if that kind of nightmare never comes crashing into your world, it's still important to be prepared and it's important to realize that difficulties of all shapes and sizes will challenge your faith and your marriage.

Any kind of hardship can take a toll on your marriage. For example-financial strain, stress at work, frequent travel with work, difficulty with kids, major illness, broken trust, moving or problems with extended family. These are some common issues that cause a husband and wife to argue or pull away from one another. The truth is that the hard times are when we need each other the most.

There have been several times, in our own marriage of fifteen years, that we've experienced various forms of hardship. In the grand scheme of things, ours weren't major, but we both felt the strain, nonetheless. One tough season that comes to mind happened about six years ago when we decided to move states. We were willingly leaving a place that we loved, but very excited about starting our new adventure in a new place. The moment we got there, Ashley felt loneliness creeping in. We were staying in a tiny rental house right beside some water and that was especially hard for her since we had two extremely loud and active small boys who couldn't swim. I was busy at my new job and Ashley was trying to hold down the fort at home with two small children. As the months slowly crept by, Ashley and I both felt weary and uncomfortable with our new city. It was a tough adjustment. There were even times when Ashley was a bit resentful towards me because it seemed like I was adjusting so much better than she was. Even still, Ashley continued to trudge on through the long days at home with our restless boys—feeling a bit lost and alone.

The tension between us began to rise because we gradually stopped being intentional about telling each other our true feelings about the move. I think both of us were so exhausted at the end of the day that we just couldn't even find the words. Eventually, this bad habit caught up with us. We both became so edgy towards one another and we weren't prioritizing date nights or time together like we once did.

The relational dynamic between us was becoming more sinister by the day. We wanted things to be better. We wanted to love where we were living. But Ashley was so homesick and frustrated with the state of things.

I remember coming to Ashley with tired eyes one day. I grabbed Ashley's hands and said, "Sweetie, this has been a really hard move for both of us. I don't know why, but it just is. What do you think would make things better for us?" She was so relieved to hear me say those words. She wasn't alone in her frustration. I felt it too. Tears welled up in her eyes as she poured out her heart to me. She told me how much she missed her friends and family. She expressed her frustration with the boys not listening. She asked me how things were going at work and I talked about some frustrations I was experiencing there. Neither of us held anything back. It felt so good to just let it all out and to call this season what it really was—HARD. It was good to know that we both had each other's back.

Friends, when we are going through a tough season—and we all will at some time or another, we must resist the urge to face it alone and allow resentment to take hold of our heart. This will help you to endure this hard season and keep your marriage strong.

We need to go to our wife and tell her what's on our mind and heart. Tell her everything—the good, the bad and the ugly. And then ask your wife to do the same. When you both do this, you will feel the weight being lifted off your shoulders. The two of you are on the same team. You win together or lose together. You lean on one another through thick and thin. That's what your marriage commitment is all about.
Your hard season may linger, but you can make it through when you face it together—hand-in-hand, heart-to-heart, day-by-day and step-by-step.

If your marriage is going through a "for worse" season right now, here are a few things we've learned to remember in those challenging seasons of life. These truths have helped us and we pray they help you as well:

1. REMEMBER THAT YOUR CHARACTER SHOULD ALWAYS BE STRONGER THAN YOUR CIRCUMSTANCES.

We can't always control what happens to us, but we can always control how we choose to respond. In those moments when I choose to stop complaining and instead give thanks to God for the good in my life, the parts that seem bad start to seem much less significant. Choose to keep a positive attitude and thankful heart regardless of what you're going through.

"Rejoice always, pray continually, give thanks in all circumstances; for this is God's will for you in Christ Jesus." *1 Thessalonians 5:16-18*

2. REMEMBER THAT YOUR STRUGGLES ALWAYS LEAD TO STRENGTH.

Every difficulty in your life, whether big or small, is something God will use to produce more strength, faith and perseverance in you-if you let Him! All your pain has a purpose.

"And we know that in all things God works for the good of those who love him, who have been called according to his purpose." *Romans 8:28*

3. REMEMBER THAT GOD'S TIMING IS ALWAYS PERFECT.

God's plans are almost always different from our plans, but His plans are always perfect! Have the patience to wait on His timing instead of forcing your own.

"For I know the plans I have for you declares the Lord; plans to prosper you and not to harm you, plans to give you hope and a future." *Jeremiah 29:11*

4. REMEMBER THAT GOD WILL NEVER LEAVE YOUR SIDE.

You may feel like you're going through struggles all alone, but from the moment you ask Jesus to bring you into God's family, He will be by your side to the end. So never lose hope!

"Be strong and courageous. Do not be afraid or terrified because of them, for the Lord your God goes with you; he will never leave you nor forsake you." *Deuteronomy 31:61*

WHEN
LIFE
IS
GOOD

We expect marriage to be hard when times are hard. However, when we say, "for better or for worse," most of us are thinking that in the good times there won't really be any struggles. Ironically, success has probably ended as many marriages as tragedy has. I know that may sound crazy, so let me explain.

Ashley and I read a news story recently about a married couple in Kentucky who won the lottery. It was the "happiest day of their lives." They played the lottery everyday and always dreamed about what they'd do if they won. Finally, their numbers came up. In a single moment, they had gone from being flat broke to millionaires! Instantly, everything changed. At first, it was amazing. They were riding the wave of adrenaline and buying everything they wanted. But it wasn't too long before the rush wore off and everything started to crumble. They began to fight about what to do with the money, which led them to become secretive and distrusting of each other. They began to develop some unhealthy habits because their new wealth gave them the false feeling of invincibility. Ultimately, this "happiest day of their lives," turned to tragedy.

Several short years after winning, the wife was dead of a drug overdose and the husband had become a paranoid recluse in his home. The one statement the newspaper was able to get from him was the sobering warning, "It ruined everything. I wouldn't wish this money on anyone." The money wasn't the problem. The money just amplified the problems they already had and also created some new ones. That might not keep you from trying to get rich quick, but hopefully it will give you some valuable perspective on life whether you end up rich or broke. People are always more important that possessions and your commitment to your spouse must always be stronger than your circumstances.

When a couple doesn't have their relationship built on faith and commitment, then it is just built on feelings or convenience. Great success can actually expose the weak spots of a marriage because it will ultimately reveal our secret motives and the level of our faith. You must never allow any set of circumstances to become more powerful in your life than your unwavering commitment to your spouse. Whether you're currently in a "better" or "worse" set of circumstances, choose to trust God and support one another. Don't let worry rob you of your peace. Find strength in each other and in the truth of God's promises.

"Don't worry about anything; instead, pray about everything. Tell God what you need, and thank him for all he has done. Then you will experience God's peace, which exceeds anything we can understand. His peace will guard your hearts and minds as you live in Christ Jesus."
Philippians 4:6-7

LIVING THE THIRD PROMISE:

"I LOVE YOU FOR BETTER OR FOR WORSE"

We pray you never have to experience the type of tragedy in your marriage that Jay and Mandra endured. But if you do, I pray that you respond with the faith and unity that they courageously showed. When you exchanged your vows and said, "For better or for worse," what you were really saying is, "I'm going to be by your side no matter what." No matter what life throws your way, you need to be able to say to your spouse, "In good times, I'm going to celebrate with you. In tragic times, I'm going to cry with you. In uncertain times, I'm going to hold you. I'm going to be by your side now and always, no matter what!"

DAY THREE

—

Activity

Start a conversation with your wife where you discuss some of the biggest struggles you've faced in your past and in your present. Then, discuss how you would both hope to respond over specific struggles in your future. Ask and answer these questions:

1. What was the biggest struggle you faced before we got married? How did you overcome it?

2. What do you believe is the biggest struggle we have overcome in our marriage?

3. What is the biggest struggle we are facing in our marriage right now?

4. How do you hope we would respond if we went bankrupt?

5. How do you hope we would respond if one of us was diagnosed with a serious illness?

6. How can I help you through the struggles you're facing?

7. How can we be better partners in facing our struggles as a team?

What did I learn about my spouse today?

What did I learn about my myself today?

As a result of what I'm learning, I'm committing to take the following actions to strengthen my marriage-

_____

_____

_____

_____

_____

_____

_____

_____

_____

_____

_____

_____

_____

_____

_____

_____

_____

Today, my prayer for my marriage is-

_____

_____

_____

_____

_____

_____

_____

_____

_____

_____

_____

_____

_____

_____

_____

_____

_____

_____

DAY FOUR
___

"FOR RICHER OR FOR POORER"

Stress related to money is one of the biggest causes of divorce. When the finances are unstable, it can make the entire marriage feel unstable. One reason couples often fight about money is the fact that one partner is a "spender" while the other is a "saver." Naturally this can cause spouses to argue. No matter the scenario, any couple can find themselves under financial pressure from time to time.

My parents struggled financially in the early years of my life but they still managed to give me some very memorable gifts. They bought me my first bicycle, my first Nintendo and even a New Kids on the Block cassette tape. Most of those gifts ended up in a dumpster, but several gifts have endured through the years and made a permanent impact on my life and faith. Among those enduring gifts was the gift of growing up with two parents who truly loved and supported each other. My parents are very financially successful today, but there was a time when my family was very poor. The economy was terrible and like many young parents, my Mom and Dad were struggling to make ends meet.

One day, Dad came home and found Mom crying while holding her crying baby. She has always been a very tenderhearted woman, but she almost never cried, so Dad knew something was terribly wrong. He asked what was going on. Through her tears she pointed to the refrigerator and said, "There's no milk and there's no money to buy more."

My parents, who are two of the hardest-working and most resourceful people on the planet, found themselves looking into the eyes of their hungry children. They felt the desperation of not knowing how to provide their most basic needs. Dad looked through the house for any spare change, but there was none to be found. There was no credit card. There was no cash. There was simply nothing.

Dad had a thought and rushed into his bedroom. He opened his sock drawer and pulled out two shiny silver dollars. They had been given to him by his Great Grandmother when he was a young boy. They were all he had left of her memory, but despite their great sentimental value (and possibly great financial value as well), their only value was that they represented meeting a need for his family. Without hesitation, Dad walked to the store, grabbed a gallon of milk and slapped those two silver dollars on the counter. That's what love looks like. Loving your spouse "for richer or for poorer" means being willing to make selfless sacrifices to provide for your family.

I told this story in a sermon at church recently and my parents happened to be sitting in the crowd. I got to the end and found myself gripped by emotion as I reflected on a lifetime of love and support I've received from them both. I looked down and saw that they were crying too. I told them I loved them. When I looked back up, I noticed that most everyone else in the crowd was crying too. Most people have a pretty ugly "cry face." I know I look like something out of a horror movie when I start crying, but this was, undoubtedly, a beautiful moment.

Mom and Dad have loved and supported each other through every season of their marriage. Since those early struggles, they've had great financial prosperity, but their values have remained completely unwavering whether they've been in a "richer" or a "poorer" state. Their example has taught me to have a healthy view of money, but even more importantly, their love for each other is what gave me a healthy view of marriage. I'm truly thankful for their continuing legacy of faith, family and love.

GOD WANTS YOU TO HAVE A HEALTHY VIEW OF MONEY

___

Whether or not your parents set a positive example for you, it's so important that you learn a healthy view of finances. So much marital stress can be traced back to financial stress. Whether you're rich or poor, developing a unified financial plan with your spouse can bring freedom and peace to your marriage. My friends Mike and Allie are living proof!

Mike and Allie were living "The American Dream," which basically means they were living beyond their means. This young family was buried in debt and trying to keep their heads above water on a schoolteacher's salary. The debt was creating stress that was putting a heavy strain on their marriage and young family. They decided that something had to change, so they took action. They researched the Bible's timeless wisdom on finances and they adjusted their spending, saving and giving accordingly. A few years later, they had experienced a dramatic turnaround and are now debt free! They're living in a freedom that they never had before and now they coach others to help them discover the same financial freedom and peace.

Jesus taught more about money than He talked about Heaven and Hell. He knew that a healthy view of money would be vital to developing a healthy view of life and marriage. If we could sum up the Bible's many teachings on money into one statement, we'd say it's, "Money is a good servant, but a poor master."

Early in our marriage, Ashley and I made some rookie mistakes when it came to money. We took on unnecessary debt, overspent and didn't save. Those decisions created a lot of stress that wise choices could have prevented. We finally learned that a commitment to financial freedom can create freedom and peace to all other aspects of life and marriage. Here are the principles that we wish we had practiced from the very beginning:

1. RELENTLESSLY ELIMINATE YOUR DEBT.

Financial debt has caused more fights between husbands and wives than nearly any other subject. It can have a suffocating impact because it removes options and replaces your freedoms with constraints. Do whatever you can do to remove debt and then avoid taking on new debt. Remember that a new car smell is nice, but it's nothing compared the debt-free scent of a paid for car!

"The rich rule over the poor, and the borrower is slave to the lender." *Proverbs 22:7*

2. WISELY PLAN YOUR SPENDING.

For a lot of people, the word "budget" is a bad word that makes their skin crawl just to speak it. To be completely transparent with you, I've always been bad at budgeting, but over the years, I've come to see the benefit of developing a spending plan. A budget is simply a way of telling your money where to go instead of watching your money fly out the window. It puts you back in control which brings peace and helps you discover that you don't actually need a lot of the stuff you've been buying.

"Then Jesus said to them, "Watch out! Be on your guard against all kinds of greed; life does not consist in an abundance of possessions." *John 12:15*

3. SYSTEMATICALLY PRIORITIZE YOUR SAVING.

There is more peace in my marriage when we have a little financial cushion in the bank. It gives reassurance to my wife that if an unexpected expense comes our way, we won't have to go sell one of our kidneys on the black market to cover it. When you save a little money out of every check, you'll be building a nest egg that will remove unnecessary stress from your marriage.

"Dishonest money dwindles away, but whoever gathers money little by little makes it grow." *Proverbs 13:11*

4. JOYFULLY INCREASE YOUR GIVING.

For all our many financial mistakes in those early years of marriage, Ashley and I did do one thing right when it came to our finances. We chose to follow the Bible's clear teaching to tithe (give the first 10% of our income to fund Christian ministry) and to be generous to those in need. That choice has brought more blessing to us than I can describe and I hope you will also experience the joy that generosity brings. The happiest couples I know are extremely generous and the most miserable couples I know are misers. Don't be a Scrooge! When you're wise with your money, it will put you in the position to be generous with your money and generosity always brings joy.

"Each of you should give what you have decided in your heart to give, not reluctantly or under compulsion, for God loves a cheerful giver." *2 Corinthians 9:7*

5. ETERNALLY MAXIMIZE YOUR INVESTMENTS.

It's important to have a retirement plan, but it's even more important to invest into causes that will create an eternal legacy. Don't just think of your money in terms of what you'll do with it from paycheck to paycheck; plan out what you'll do with your money that will impact generations to come. When your money is in the right place, your heart will be in the right place.

"Do not store up for yourselves treasures on earth, where moths and vermin destroy, and where thieves break in and steal. But store up for yourselves treasures in heaven, where moths and vermin do not destroy, and where thieves do not break in and steal. For where your treasure is, there your heart will be also." *Matthew 6:19-21*

THE
MYTH
OF
"MORE"

When our oldest son, Cooper, was born, somebody gave us a DVD of baby sign language that we started showing him when he was just a few months old. As new parents, we had no idea what we were doing, but we thought that if our baby learned sign language, then everybody would think that we really knew our stuff! The DVD didn't make him a fluent phenomenon in signing, but it did teach him something. It turned out there was one sign that he picked up and consistently used. He knew what it meant and he used it often. It was the sign for the word "more." Before he could speak a word, he had already discovered the instinctive human fascination with more.

As a baby, you just want more milk or more toys, but as we grow, the hunger for more grows. In adulthood, most of us are fueled by the drive for more money, more success, more pleasure, more fun, more rest, more sex and more of pretty much everything else. Our materialistic, hedonistic culture convinces us that we're not happy, but if we just buy a little more of a certain product, then we will be. It's a vicious cycle that never ends until we discover a life changing principle from the truth of God's word.

Here's the truth: "more" will never make you happy. It's a myth. It's an empty pursuit. Contentment isn't a result of having more; it's a result of wanting less. Until you're content with what you've already got, you won't be content no matter how much you get! God wants you to live in a spirit of gratitude and contentment. Don't let the selfishness of this world rob you of that. Choose to give thanks in all circumstances and be truly content with what you already have and the "more" that comes your way will just be the icing on the cake. God has many more blessings in store for you, but you won't be able to fully embrace them until you're willing to trade more of this world for more of God. If you are willing to apply these principles to your faith and your finances, your marriage will be stronger no matter how much money you happen to have in the bank.

THE SECRET TO REAL CONTENT- MENT

___

It's so easy to fall into the trap of thinking more money would instantly fix all of our problems, but it's not the case. King Solomon is proof! Solomon was one of the wealthiest, wisest and most successful people to ever live. He literally had anything and everything he desired, except for one thing...happiness. The Book of Ecclesiastes in the Bible records Solomon's frustrations:

"I denied myself nothing my eyes desired; I refused my heart no pleasure. My heart took delight in all my labor and this was the reward for all my toil. Yet when I surveyed all that my hands had done and what I had toiled to achieve, everything was meaningless, a chasing after the wind; nothing was gained under the sun." *Ecclesiastes 2:10-11*

Solomon's problem started when he strayed away from God's design for marriage as being a lifelong, committed, monogamous partnership to one person and allowed his culture to redefine his views. He ended up with hundreds of wives and hundreds more concubines. He thought sex, success and stuff would make him happy, but it never did.

The deepest longings of your heart can only be fulfilled when you make the countercultural choice to trust God's plan for your life and your marriage. His plans for you and your marriage are perfect and whether you're facing good times or bad, for better or for worse, you and your spouse can discover true contentment.

You can come to understand the words of the Apostle Paul who said, "I know how to live on almost nothing or with everything. I have learned the secret of living in every situation, whether it is with a full stomach or empty, with plenty or little. For I can do everything through Christ, who gives me strength." *Philippians 4:12-13*

LIVING THE FOURTH PROMISE:

"I WILL LOVE YOU FOR RICHER OR FOR POORER"

If there's not peace in your finances right now, make a plan of action to start in a new direction. Don't live beyond your means. Refuse to allow financial stress (whether pressure from a lack of resources or greed from an abundance of resources) to rob you of joy and contentment. Work together to create goals for debt reduction and generosity. Dream about ways to create a legacy for future generations through your finances, your faith and your love for one another.

DAY FOUR

Activity

Take an assessment of your current financial situation. Talk about things you're doing well and things you'd like to re-prioritize. Each of you choose one financial goal you'd like to achieve in the next year and also one financial goal you'd like to achieve in your lifetimes. Dream about how life could look once those goals are achieved. Talk about specific ways you could start moving towards those goals. Don't blame each other for your current financial strains. Find ways to work together to bring solutions. If you and your spouse are in financial strain right now, please know that there is hope.

Even if you owe hundreds of thousands of dollars in debt and dread getting your statements every month, you can still set a budget and gradually pay it off. Some great resources can be found at DaveRamsey.com. There are also some amazing apps out there that make budgeting much easier. One free app we would recommend is called "Every Dollar." If this website or app doesn't seem like your speed, you can always set up an appointment with a local financial planner. Whatever you choose, just make sure you take immediate action and stick to your plan together. You can do this!

What did I learn about my spouse today?

_____

_____

_____

_____

_____

_____

_____

_____

_____

_____

_____

_____

_____

_____

_____

_____

_____

What did I learn about my myself today?

As a result of what I'm learning, I'm committing to take the following actions to strengthen my marriage-

_____

_____

_____

_____

_____

_____

_____

_____

_____

_____

_____

_____

_____

_____

_____

Today, my prayer for my marriage is-

DAY FIVE
___

"FOR-
SAKING
ALL
OTHERS"

Life was good for Jason and Jennifer. They had just had their first child a few months earlier. They had that look of both excitement and exhaustion that all new parents seem to have. Life seemed to be rolling along just fine for them until the day a bombshell dropped that nobody saw coming.

Jason gave me a call late one night and told me that he had to talk to me. I could sense the urgency in his voice, which was out of character because he was typically the most laid back guy I knew. My own heart was racing as I drove to meet with him. I had no idea what to expect and I was shocked by the news he was about to give me.

With tears in his eyes, he started to tell me a story that I knew was not going to have a happy ending. He talked about this young woman at work who had been a good friend to him. They would work long hours with each other and really felt a close connection. She was married too, but didn't seem happy in her marriage. At this point, I knew where the story was heading, yet I let him finish telling it.

Their friendship escalated and their conversations began to deepen to personal issues. Those close conversations led to hugs which led to...well, you probably know the rest. He cheated on his wife. He was desperate for a way to fix this mess. His wife already knew and the joy she had been feeling over dreaming of their family's future came crashing down in a single moment. His life seemed like it was over.
As I listened to him talk, I honestly didn't know whether I should give him a hug to encourage him or punch him in the face for being an idiot. I decided to hug him. I had seen this familiar scene play in the lives of others and I knew his consequences were going to be painful enough without me adding to them.

In the months that followed, he made drastic steps to rebuild his broken marriage and regain his wife's trust. I met with him regularly for accountability and support. He cut off all conversation with the other woman and even sought a job transfer so that he wouldn't be near her. He knew that putting distance between him and this other woman was the only way for his marriage to have a chance of survival. The survival of their marriage is a miracle that can only be explained by the grace of God. Even in that victory, there is a sad reality that their marriage will never be the same. Even with great days ahead, there will always be deep scars and damaged trust.

AN AFFAIR-PROOF MARRIAGE

Almost daily we see the devastating results of adultery in people's lives. It destroys marriages and families. It causes vast emotional scars on everyone who is involved, including the children. While it is possible to forgive and move forward, it is so much better to never make this mistake in the first place.

When you made your vow to 'forsake all others," you were promising your spouse that there would be no one who would ever take their rightful place in your mind, your heart, your life or your bed! That commitment must be a daily focus and you must remain vigilant of any dangerous behavior that could lead you down that path. We often assume that having an affair is sleeping with someone other than our spouse, but an affair occurs anytime we choose to prioritize someone or something else over our spouse and put our marriage on the back burner. Most of the time, this begins innocently, so it's important for us to understand what can take us out of bounds. Here are four common ways you might be tempted to have an affair. Please safeguard your marriage from all four!

1. FAILURE TO CREATE HEALTHY BOUNDARIES WITH FEMALE CO-WORKERS/FRIENDS/ACQUAINTANCES.

It's important to note that people rarely set out to have an affair. It usually starts fairly innocently and it begins when we fail to set healthy boundaries for working relationships and social exchanges with women. We need to be keenly aware of what we share with women through conversation. If we're not careful, we can place ourselves in a vulnerable position through conversations with women that we find are easy to talk to. We can end up sharing our hearts with a woman who isn't our wife and this opens the door to intimacy. We start thinking about her more and look forward to sharing more conversations and time with her. We start placing ourselves in dangerous territory and before we even realize it, we find ourselves in an emotional and sometimes physical affair.

2. ALLOWING YOUR FRIENDS OR CO-WORKERS TO DICTATE YOUR MARRIAGE.

This may seem like a stretch to some of you, but sadly we have seen marriages end due to a husband surrounding himself with friends who have no respect for his wife and encourage him to be with them instead of investing in his marriage. We often become like the people we hang with the most, so it is extremely important that we choose our friends wisely. We must also remember that we shouldn't be spending more time with our friends than we do with our wife. And, if we are, we need to be intentional about changing this as soon as possible.

3. SEEKING SEXUAL SATISFACTION FROM ANYONE OR ANYTHING OTHER THAN YOUR WIFE.

We are sexual beings, so let me be clear here—there is absolutely nothing wrong with fantasizing about your spouse. Sex is a beautiful and important part of marriage and it should be enjoyable for both the husband and the wife. But we open ourselves up to having an emotional and/or sexual affair when we allow other people into our fantasy through things like porn, checking out other women, erotica, sexually explicit romance novels and even certain television programs. We may tell ourselves that we aren't affected by these, but the honest truth is we are. Porn and sexually explicit writing change the way we think about sex and the expectations we have for our wife. Instead of allowing these counterfeit sexual fantasies into our bedroom, talk to your wife about your desires, needs and expectations for your sex life. Be honest and open with one another. This is a major step towards real intimacy.

4. KEEPING SECRETS FROM YOUR WIFE AND NOT CONSULTING HER ON DAILY DECISIONS.

Secrets start small. We tell ourselves things like:

"She doesn't really need to know about this one little conversation with a female co-worker."

"It's not a big deal that I have a secret account and buy stuff she doesn't know about."

"Why can't I have password on my phone? She doesn't need to know every time I get a text."

"This is my life. I'm a grown man. I don't have to tell her everything."

If we are honest, I think most of us can admit to at least one of these statements crossing our mind a time or two. These seemingly little or harmless secrets will come back to bite us. What was once a little thing can blow up in our face and turn into a full blown affair. And the longer we keep secrets, the easier it becomes for us to keep bigger secrets. Then, before we know it, we become nothing more than two married roommates. It doesn't have to be this way. You can turn things around by being open, honest and vulnerable with your wife and you can start today!

WHEN TRUST IS BROKEN

Maybe your marriage has faced the terrible scars of infidelity or maybe you've done a great job building an affair-proof marriage. Either way, almost every marriage has encountered difficulties over broken trust. Infidelity is broader than just having an affair (though that is a common and destructive example); infidelity is the breakdown of the fidelity or trust in your marriage.

Trust is a tricky thing. It is the foundation of every healthy marriage. It is the security that makes intimacy possible. It can be simultaneously strong and yet very fragile. It takes great effort and time to build, but it can be broken quickly.

Perhaps this issue has plagued your marriage. Maybe an instance from the past has never been fully resolved, so there's an underlying tension in the marriage. Maybe secrets are being kept and those secrets are creating an invisible barrier keeping your marriage from moving forward. Whether your marriage has rock-solid trust, or you're currently reeling from a breach of trust, these principles can add value to your marriage.

Here are some important principles to help you build trust in your marriage or rebuild it if it's been broken:

1. DON'T KEEP SECRETS.

In marriage, secrets are as dangerous as lies. Never have a conversation you wouldn't want her to hear, view a website you wouldn't want her to see or go someplace you wouldn't want her to know about. Complete transparency is vital to building complete trust.

2. RECOGNIZE THE DIFFERENCE BETWEEN FORGIVENESS AND TRUST.

Forgiveness and trust are two different things. When you've been wronged, you should give forgiveness instantly (which is grace), but you should give your trust slowly (which is common sense). Forgiveness by its very nature cannot be earned; it can only be given. Trust by its very nature cannot be given; it can only be earned. Forgiveness has to come first and then grace can pave the way to restoration and renewed trust.

3. DON'T RETALIATE.

When we've been wronged, we usually have an urge to punish the person who wronged us. We want this person to feel the pain that he or she caused us, but this kind of thinking hurts everyone involved and damages trust even more. It's been said, "Holding a grudge is like drinking poison and then hoping the other person dies!" When you've been wronged in a marriage, give clear and specific guidelines for how trust can be restored, but don't punish the other person in the process.

4. BE CONSISTENT.

When you are rebuilding trust, do your best to be consistent in your words and your actions. Consistency brings security and security eventually brings trust.

5. BE WILLING TO TEMPORARILY GIVE UP SOME FREEDOMS.

When an arm is broken, it has to be put in a cast to restrict its motion so it can have time to heal. When you've broken trust, you must be willing to temporarily give up certain freedoms and accept certain restrictions to allow time for healing. This is usually the most uncomfortable part of the process, but it's vital.

6. KEEP THE LOVE ALIVE.

The Bible says that, "Love covers over a multitude of sins." I love that picture of love being strong enough to cover our imperfections and fill in the cracks of our broken hearts. Keep loving each other and allow God to use the power of love and grace to bring wholeness and healing to your marriage.

LIVING THE FIFTH PROMISE:

"I WILL LOVE YOU FAITHFULLY; FORSAKING ALL OTHERS"

We protect everything that's important to us. We lock our houses and our cars because we don't want them stolen or vandalized. We keep our money in the bank because they have a vault and armed guards. If it's valuable, we protect it from anyone who would harm it.

You need to see your marriage as a priceless treasure that must be protected at all costs. There are many in the world that would steal it or harm it and you are responsible for keeping it safe. Do whatever you can to build safeguards around your marriage and specifically, do everything in your power to protect your marriage from adultery!

Make every effort to build an affair-proof marriage. Come clean about any secrets you've been keeping from your spouse including pornography. Build your marriage on a foundation of trust. When trust has been broken, work together to promote forgiveness, healing and time to rebuild trust.

DAY FIVE

Activity

Today's activity is designed to help you determine the current level of trust in your marriage and discover ways to build trust and keep it strong. Trust is the foundation of every healthy relationship. We treat trust like it's a mystical, hard-to-define concept, but it's actually very concrete. I believe this simple explanation of the process of building trust can be a helpful tool for you to measure the current trust in your relationship and also to understand how to take trust to a deeper level. Stronger trust always creates stronger relationships.

Trust defined: "Trust is a choice to be available, vulnerable and transparent in a relationship because the person you're trusting has proven worthy of your partnership through consistency in their honesty, integrity and dependability."

Based on this simple definition of trust, we see that trust is much more than a gut feeling or a blind faith in someone. It's merit-based. For this reason, trust is completely different than love and forgiveness. Love and forgiveness can't be earned (only given freely), but trust can't be given freely; it must be earned. Trust is the only vital part of a relationship that must be earned. We don't have to trust someone in order to love or forgive them but love and forgiveness are vital to allowing trust to have the opportunity to be rebuilt when it's been broken.

Here's how trust works in every relationship. These are the Six Stages of Trust, understanding these will help you strengthen your marriage:

STAGE 1: CONNECTION

When you and your wife first met, there was a connection and you subconsciously started on the first stage of building trust. We're drawn to someone and feel a connection which propels us to start the process of building a relationship. You then proceeded to step two by cautiously moving forward.

STAGE 2: CAUTION*

We cautiously start to pursue the possibility of trust in this fledgling relationship. We start creating opportunities where we can observe this person's character in action and allow them to view the same in us. We're careful to proceed with caution and patience because the process of building trust is delicate and it requires time.

*Whenever trust is broken in a relationship, we must always return to this second stage and proceed with caution to allow trust to be rebuilt through the remaining stages. Remember that forgiveness and trust are two different things. Forgiveness should be given freely because grace can't be earned, but trust can't be given freely; it can only be earned. If trust has been broken in your marriage, you both must return to Stage 2 and start rebuilding from there.

STAGE 3: CONSISTENCY

This is where trust truly begins to build (or rebuild). Consistency is the primary ingredient of trust. When we observe consistency in honest words and actions from someone, we naturally let our guard down and can experience the deeper levels of relational intimacy trust always makes possible. Their consistency gives us the courage to take the next step.

STAGE 4: COURAGE

Trust is rooted in viewing consistency in another person, but it still requires an element of faith and courage. This is the point in the marriage where we're ready to put our heart on the line. We're willing to assume some risk (which is required in every relationship) because we now feel safe and secure with her.

STAGE 5: COMMITMENT

Our courage to trust always leads to a commitment. Every relationship requires some level of commitment and the level of our commitment will ultimately define the level of our relationship. This is more pronounced in a marriage relationship where the commitment is a sacred, lifelong vow, but even in friendship and business relationships, some level of commitment is always required. Are you both fully and wholeheartedly committed to building trust in the marriage?

STAGE 6: COMFORT

When you truly trust someone, you'll know it's because you'll feel completely safe and comfortable with them. They've earned your trust and you've freely given it. You don't doubt their actions or motives. You choose to believe the best in them because they've consistently shown you the best in themselves. When you get to this stage of trust, you've found something priceless and precious, so make sure you do everything in your power to keep it! If someone has done everything to earn your trust, but you still don't have comfort, it may be because of trust issues in your life or scars from your past that you need to explore on your own to find healing. Don't punish the people in your life for wounds inflicted by others long ago. Find healing and peace so you can wholeheartedly trust again. Trust is the foundation of every healthy marriage.

So, take some time and discuss the current level of trust in your marriage. Are you at Stage 6 Trust? If not, what's holding you back? Work to build trust and fight to keep it once you have it. The strength of your trust in each other will determine the strength of your marriage.

What did I learn about my spouse today?

What did I learn about my myself today?

As a result of what I'm learning, I'm committing to take the following actions to strengthen my marriage-

_____

_____

_____

_____

_____

_____

_____

_____

_____

_____

_____

_____

_____

_____

_____

_____

_____

Today, my prayer for my marriage is-

_____

_____

_____

_____

_____

_____

_____

_____

_____

_____

_____

_____

_____

_____

_____

_____

_____

DAY
SIX

"IN SICKNESS AND IN HEALTH"

Our friends, John and Dawn, are an amazing married couple. They laugh together, they dream together, they support each other and on top of all that, their names even rhyme! They're the kind of people who light up a room the moment they walk through the door.

John has enjoyed a great deal of success in the corporate world and Dawn has devoted much of her time and energy to philanthropy. They both are extremely talented and also generous with their time, talents and resources. The world is truly a better place because of them both. They've always had big dreams and big plans for the future but those plans were recently changed in a way they never could've expected.

A few years ago, this happy couple was dealt a devastating blow which would rock them to the core. Dawn was a healthy and vibrant woman in her mid-forties, barely half-way through the life she had mapped out in her mind, when the doctor gave her the news. She was diagnosed with Multiple Sclerosis which is a debilitating and life-limiting illness. The disease slowly and painfully removes a person's mobility and ultimately leads to death.

John and Dawn were stopped in their tracks. Their plans for the future instantly and irreversibly changed. This diagnosis was going to be the biggest test their faith and their marriage had ever experienced. These past few years have been incredibly challenging for them both, but I've stood in awe at their faith in God and their love for one another as they've beautifully lived out their vow, "In sickness and in health."

The disease has slowly and systematically robbed Dawn of her physical vibrancy and freedoms. She is now confined to a wheelchair and the tedious process of preparing to the leave the house has gone from fifteen minutes when she was healthy, to an ordeal that can now last five hours or more. Through it all, there have been many tears shed by both of them, but they've never given up on each other.

The tenderness with which John cares for her physical needs is awe-inspiring. The appreciation and affirmation Dawn gives to John is beautiful. The faith they both have in God is unshakable. They stand in faith knowing God's promises are true and even if physical healing doesn't come in this lifetime, eternal healing will come through faith in Christ.

In the meantime, they face each day together. They are completely united in the struggle. The disease may be Dawn's diagnosis, but the struggle belongs to them both. Watching them courageously face this struggle together has inspired me and countless others. I pray God would continue to give them strength and grace for the road ahead and I pray that if Ashley and I ever face a similar challenge, we'll have the faith to face it like John and Dawn!

WHEN LIFE FEELS BROKEN

———

One of the greatest challenges a marriage can face is when illness strikes. We often assume major illness or injury won't be an issue for us until very late in life, but injury and illness can strike without warning. The physical, emotional and financial strain they create can threaten to put a wedge between a husband and wife. Sometimes the most debilitating aspect of the illness comes in the form of discouragement. You can feel the dream you had for your life and marriage has been stolen or broken beyond repair. In those moments of pain and discouragement, you need to remember an important lesson that I learned at Christmas time in a very unlikely way.

Christmas can be "the most wonderful time of the year," but the holidays can also have a way of making life's regrets, struggles and brokenness seem even bigger. Maybe this Christmas you will find yourself in a difficult place. You look around at your life and you're overwhelmed with frustration and disappointment about how things are turning out. You feel like every happy Christmas song is rubbing salt into the wounds of your heart. If any of that sounds familiar to you, I want to share a quick story that completely changed my perspective and perhaps it can change yours too.

A couple of years ago my family and I were braving the Christmas craziness at Walmart when my kids passed a display of gingerbread houses and started begging, "Daddy, PLEASE, PLEASE can we get a gingerbread house?" My mind started drifting to the magical holiday memories we'd make together sitting around the table sipping hot cocoa, while making the world's most perfect gingerbread house. It would look just as perfect as the one on the box. I gave in and pulled out the eight bucks to buy it and we headed home to make some Christmas magic.

On the way home, the boys started fighting over the gingerbread house box in the back of the van. By the time we got home and opened up the box, all that was left inside were broken pieces. I was so frustrated! My perfect plan was as broken as the pieces of that gingerbread house. I went to throw the whole box in the trash when Ashley stopped me and asked, "What are you doing?" "I'm going to throw this thing away! It's broken! It's never going to look like the picture on the box!" I exclaimed. She smiled and replied with such patience and wisdom, "It doesn't have to look like the picture on the box." She took the box from my hands and placed it on the table and pulled out all those broken pieces and we started making oddly-shaped-but-beautiful gingerbread cookies. We laughed and had more fun together that night than we'd had in a long time. I almost missed it because I was going to let frustration get the best of me. Here's the point of the story...maybe your life feels like the broken pieces of that gingerbread house. You had a picture in your mind of how life was going to turn out, but now your life will never look like the picture on the box. Here's the good news...it doesn't have to! I truly believe God can take the broken pieces of our lives and create something even more beautiful than we ever could have created on our own. Trust Him with your broken pieces of your life, your health and your marriage and you'll be amazed what He can create with them!

"For I know the plans I have for you declares the LORD; plans to prosper you and not to harm you, plans to give you hope and a future." *Jeremiah 29:11*

HOW TO RESPOND WHEN YOU OR YOUR WIFE BECOMES SICK

Sickness can run the gamut from a simple cold to a life-threatening illness. In either scenario, we have an opportunity to show great love, kindness and patience to our spouse. The longer the illness, the harder it becomes. We have seen the hardship of a serious illness nearly destroy the love and respect between a couple. On the other side, I have seen couples come together with tremendous love, faith and unity to support one another and overcome the sickness.

Some of you might be fighting a major disease right now. My heart and prayers go out to you and your family. No matter what the doctors or test results tell you, I want you to know that there is hope. I love this Bible verse that poignantly speak to this issue:

> "Two are better than one,
> because they have a good return for their labor:
> If either of them falls down,
> one can help the other up.
> But pity anyone who falls
> and has no one to help them up.
> Also, if two lie down together, they will keep warm.
> But how can one keep warm alone?
> Though one may be overpowered,
> two can defend themselves.
> A cord of three strands is not quickly broken."
> *Ecclesiastes 4:9-12*

As husband and wife, we are going to experience various trials throughout our marriage-many that we never see coming. However dire it may appear, we must come together and help one another. God gave us a great gift in one another and He is with us. This "cord of three strands" as described in the verse, is you, your spouse and God. There is tremendous hope when all three are tightly intertwined.

Whether you are going through a season of illness right now or you are both currently healthy, here are seven important things to do when your spouse is sick:

1. ACKNOWLEDGE THE ILLNESS.

When our spouse is sick, the worst thing we can do is act like this problem doesn't exist. We must acknowledge the pain he/she is in and the fear that one has when facing a major illness. We need to stay close and offer encouragement but also realize that the only way we can fight the illness is to first address that the illness exists.

2. BE THERE.

If at all possible, we need to try and be at all the major appointments... especially if our spouse has requested that we be there. Sometimes it might not make sense to us, but we still need to do it. Our presence can bring peace if we let it. We can be there to physically take care of them, pray with them, hold their hand, console them and even cry with them if they receive some bad test results. We need to be present to remind our spouse how much we love him/her and that we aren't going to leave his/her side through this struggle.

3. LIGHTEN THE LOAD.

When we are facing a dangerous upcoming surgery or intense treatment, the fear and anxiety that ensues can be overwhelming. No matter which partner is going through the illness, it can affect both. As the healthy spouse, we need to try and bear the load with our spouse as much as possible. When he/she is having a particularly hard day with pain and anxiety, we need to try and get him/her out of the house. Sometimes we just need to create a diversion like going to a movie, eating lunch at his/her favorite restaurant, or taking a walk outside to get some fresh air. It's okay to laugh together. Laughter and smiles are good for the soul. Other times, we just need to listen to their concerns, fears, details about the surgery or treatment. Whatever we do, our willingness to jump in and lighten the load will help our spouse to face this trial without being overtaken by the weight of it all.

4. HONOR HIS/HER REQUESTS.

In an age of social media, we can let the entire world know about every little detail of our lives with a few clicks on the computer. Facebook is a great place to ask for prayers and even needs, but we need to check with our spouse first. Recently, some friends of ours had been facing a debilitating illness and they had decided to only tell a few friends about it. They did this only because they didn't want too many people showing up at the hospital or unannounced drop-ins at their house. This may sound harsh to some of you, but I get it. Sometimes we want to put the news out there and accept the help and prayers, but other times we just want our inner circle to know. And that's okay. We have to be sensitive to what our spouse requests during this season.

5. ASK FOR HELP.

This is especially important when we are going through a long health battle with our spouse. If we face something like cancer, the treatments can last for months and even years. In order to maintain a job, family life and some sense of normalcy, we are going to need help. We can't be prideful and think that we can face all these challenges alone. We need to reach out to friends and family we trust and sometimes, that means hiring a reliable babysitter, nurse or cleaning person who can help out during this time. There is no shame in that at all, and in fact, the extra hands will allow us to spend more time with our spouse.

6. TALK ABOUT IT.

Being there, day in and day out, with a spouse who is very ill can certainly take a toll on our own mind and heart. It's important that we have safe people in our lives that we can talk to about what we are going through. This person can be a same gender friend, counselor, pastor or family member (unless a brother/sister or parent). He/she must be someone we can trust with the details of the illness as well as our feelings and someone who is encouraging and shares our faith. It's important that this safe person is our same gender only to protect us against temptation and inappropriate relationships that could be harmful to our marriage.

7. PRAY ABOUT IT.

This might be the most important one of all. When we face a serious illness, so much is unknown. We need the power of God in our lives. He is our ultimate Healer. He can give us peace that surpasses understanding and a calm in the unpredictable storm. As spouses, we need to pray together and on our own. Pray for healing, peace, strength, good news, effective medicine, successful surgeries, and support. God hears our prayers and calms our hearts. More than anything, we need to perceive this crisis of illness as an opportunity to honor our marital vow to, "Love each other in both sickness and health." God will use this to strengthen our marriage and our faith if we don't lose hope and stay strong together.

THE
RECIPE
FOR A
HEALTHY
MARRIAGE

Even if one of you becomes physically sick, your marriage can be healthy. Never lose sight of that truth. Your circumstances don't define your marriage. I want to end out today's reading with a recipe that can help your marriage stay healthy through all the ups and downs of life. Ashley and I like watching the Food Network. It usually leads to us searching the house for cupcakes. We've always enjoyed learning how chefs do their work. One of the most consistent themes in the shows is that the right ingredients make all the difference. If you put good stuff in, you'll usually get good stuff out.

In marriage, we need to sometimes see ourselves as chefs who are searching for the perfect ingredients to add while also being very mindful to keep the bad ingredients (like the "marriage-killers") far away. There are (at least) seven vital ingredients to a healthy marriage. I've seen too many couples overcompensate with an extreme focus on a few of these ingredients to makeup for the fact that they're missing something. It's like trying to bake brownies and following the instructions perfectly, but leaving out eggs or sugar. Even if everything else is perfect, it's still going to taste funny!

Let this recipe for a healthy marriage be a checklist to help you build the marriage of your dreams. The good news is that even if you're missing some of these, you can still get them! None of them are out of your reach. For a healthy, happy, vibrant, fun, exciting, encouraging, rockin' marriage-you've got to mix in the following ingredients:

1. LAUGHTER.

I believe that laughter is the lifeline of marriage. In good times and bad, you've got to be able to laugh with your spouse. A marriage with zero laughter is a sign of a marriage in deep trouble. Find reasons and ways to laugh together.

2. COMMUNICATION.

Between the two of us, my wife and I have three higher education degrees in communication and we still have to work at communicating well in our marriage. (Like most things, she's a lot better than I am.) It doesn't come naturally for anybody! Every husband and every wife has to be intentional about being a good listener and clearly communicating. Spend more time going on walks, going on drives, going out to dinner and being in settings that promote conversation.

3. SEX.

Sex is vital to a healthy marriage. It's a God-given gift to promote oneness, intimacy, and pleasure (in addition to procreation). Make sex a priority. If things are healthy in the bedroom, everything starts getting healthier.

4. FRIENDSHIPS.

In too many marriages, the wife has her set of friends and the husband has his and they rarely or never connect socially. You need couple friends that you share together. My wife and I have always had a small group through our church and those relationships have been a great source of laughter, joy and encouragement for both of us.

5. GOALS.

Couples shouldn't just plan together, they should dream together. Without common goals and dreams for each other and for your family, you will be like a ship without a compass. Dream big and help each other reach those dreams.

6. CELEBRATION.

When goals are reached or milestones achieved, spouses should celebrate it together! Your marriage should be full of moments of celebration. Celebrate together privately and find ways to celebrate life's victories and moments with your extended family and friends. Even in life's toughest seasons, there are still plenty of excuses to have a party!

7. FAITH.

If these were in order of importance, faith would easily be at the top! God invented marriage and without Him, I'm convinced that no marriage can be what He intended it to be. Pray together, study God's Word together and allow Him to direct your paths. He is the one who can hold you together even when the world feels like it's falling apart.

LIVING OUT THE SIXTH PROMISE:

"IN SICKNESS AND IN HEALTH."

Of all the vows, the promise to love "in sickness and in health," may be the most challenging because sickness can steal our energy faster than most anything else. There will be times you can live out this vow in little ways, like pampering your wife with backrubs and chicken noodle soup while they're fighting off a cold, but there may also be times you're called to stand by each other through devastating illness or injury.

If those moments of hardship come, choose to face them together. Make the ingredients of a healthy marriage a lifelong priority. Take turns being strong for one another in the moments when the other feels weak. Allow your wife to serve you in the times you're not able to take care of yourself and be willing to do the same for her. Never give up on each other!

DAY SIX
—
Activity

Building on the concept of a recipe for a happy and healthy marriage, today's activity requires a recipe. Specifically, you and your wife have to cook something together. It doesn't have to be elaborate. It can be as simple as a box of store-bought cookie mix, but you both have to participate. Stir the batter together. Crack the eggs together. Eat the cookies (or whatever you choose to make) together.

This activity serves multiple purposes. It will provide you an opportunity to talk about how the ingredients impact the finished product and you can talk about the ingredients of your own marriage and what you'd like to add to (or remove from) the current recipe. Also, some of the best conversations happen when a couple is sharing a task or activity together. If you've never been in the kitchen together working on something, you might be amazed and how fresh and unique the conversation can become in that setting.

What did I learn about my spouse today?

_____

_____

_____

_____

_____

_____

_____

_____

_____

_____

_____

_____

_____

_____

_____

_____

_____

What did I learn about my myself today?

_____

_____

_____

_____

_____

_____

_____

_____

_____

_____

_____

_____

_____

_____

_____

_____

_____

_____

_____

As a result of what I'm learning, I'm committing to take the following actions to strengthen my marriage-

_____

_____

_____

_____

_____

_____

_____

_____

_____

_____

_____

_____

_____

_____

_____

_____

_____

_____

Today, my prayer for my marriage is-

_____

_____

_____

_____

_____

_____

_____

_____

_____

_____

_____

_____

_____

_____

_____

_____

_____

_____

DAY SEVEN

"TIL DEATH DO US PART."

Harold and Louise are an extraordinary couple. Ashley and I had the privilege of meeting them at a recent marriage conference we were hosting and we were instantly drawn to them. There was a sparkle in their eyes and an adoration they obviously had for one another. They couldn't help themselves from smiling every time their eyes met. Even though they were both in their late seventies, they acted like two teenagers in love. We spent as much time around them as we could that weekend because we wanted to learn the secret of their lifelong love. I wanted to know how their love had grown richer with time and how even through painful setbacks in Louise's health, they both remained joyful, optimistic and passionately devoted to one another.

Louise shared a story with us which gave us a glimpse into their lifelong love. She said, "Our first date was on March 17, so on April 17, Harold brought me a long stem rose to celebrate our one month anniversary. I was genuinely impressed by his thoughtfulness but I didn't expect the roses to come very often. I was so surprised when he brought me another rose on May 17 to celebrate our second month together. I smiled and thought, 'Wow! This fella is a keeper!' She looked at Harold with a smile and continued her story. "After we got married, I expected the roses to stop. But on the 17th that first month of our marriage, another rose appeared."

She paused to squeeze Harold's hand and tears began to form in her eyes as she smiled and said, "It has been fifty-four years since our first date, and every month on the 17th for 648 months in a row, Harold has brought me a rose." As she finished her story, I was simultaneously inspired by their love story and at the same time feeling like an insensitive jerk for never having done anything for Ashley that could match that level of consistent thoughtfulness. Harold definitely challenged me to raise the bar in my own marriage! I obviously can't build a time machine and go back to the beginning and start that type of tradition, though I can (and you can too) start today to bring more thoughtfulness and romance to the marriage.

Harold and Louise would be quick to tell you it takes a lot more than roses to build a strong, lifelong marriage. The flowers weren't really the point of their story; it was the thoughtfulness behind the flowers. As I spend time with couples who have faithfully loved each other for decades, I'm convinced their secret is really no secret at all. It's a simple choice to put love into action by consistently serving, encouraging, supporting and adoring one another.

In this chapter, we're going to explore some practical and powerful ways to build the kind of marriage that will remain strong and vibrant through every season of life. We'll start by exploring the power of healthy habits in your marriage.

DEVELO-PING HEALTHY HABITS IN YOUR MARRIAGE

In his groundbreaking book, "The 7 Habits of Highly Effective People," Stephen Covey identified the traits which consistently cause people to rise from mediocrity to excellence. The book revealed the timeless truth that our daily habits will be what determine the course of our lives. This idea might sound revolutionary but it has been around for a long time. It was the Ancient Greek Philosopher Aristotle who said, "We are what we repeatedly do. Excellence, therefore, is not an act, but a habit."

Ashley and I have developed a healthy habit of going to the local YMCA. For us, going to the gym is more than just an opportunity to work out. It offers two hours of free childcare and for parents of three young boys, that's worth its weight in gold! One of our favorite dates happens at the Y. While our kids are playing and having fun, we spend the first thirty minutes sitting down and having a cup of coffee and talking with each other. We make sure the kids know what we're doing to plant that seed in their young minds that their Mommy and Daddy love each other and make their marriage a priority.

A lot of folks walk in ready for their workout and see us lounging on a loveseat and they sometimes give us funny looks like we're wasting our time. But for us, it's one of the most productive moments of the day. Sure, I'd probably have smaller love handles if I spent that extra half hour on the treadmill but I wouldn't trade that time with Ashley for the world. Making time for each other a consistent priority has been one of the most significant, positive decisions we've made for our marriage. Recently, a guy who works here at the YMCA made a point to stop us and tell us that his daughter and son-in-law were having marriage problems. He had told them about our little "gym date" routine and actually bought them a gym membership. He encouraged them to take advantage of the childcare not only to work out but to also work out their relationship. That was a huge compliment to us and a challenge to continue developing the types of marriage-building habits that are worth imitating. I hope it helps them as much as it has helped us.

Getting a marriage in shape isn't all that different from getting your body in shape. You don't get out of shape all at once and you won't get back into shape all at once. You can make a decision to immediately alter your course in a healthier direction. Over time, those consistent little investments into the health of your relationship will pay off huge dividends. Your love handles may not get any smaller but your love for each will grow and that's really what counts the most!

8 MUST-HAVES FOR YOUR MARRIAGE

Everybody talks about it-the must-have of the day...the week...the season. This time of year, many of us go crazy to get that important item that we just can't live without. The television tells us. Social media shows us. It's up close and in our faces. These kind of must-haves are just things that will, without a doubt, be replaced by the next, hottest must-have item of the season. There are certainly some must-haves for our marriage too.

These eight must-haves aren't anything money can buy and they can't be replaced by the next best thing. They are eternal and necessary and our marriage can't live without them. If you want your marriage to make it until the finish line, you've got to have these eight things. So, what are the must-haves for your marriage? Here they are in no particular order:

1. LOVE.

This word gets tossed around a lot. In marriage, love takes on a deeper meaning than the love we feel for shoes or animals. We pledge our undying love to each other on our wedding day. It carries great weight with it. Love requires commitment — not just a feeling and it is rooted in truth and transparency. Love is intentional. We can't decide to love our spouse one day and not the next. It takes work just like tending to a garden. Love is an action that both partners must choose to do daily.

2. RESPECT.

Have you ever been around a couple who obviously don't respect each other? It's painful, right? How can two people who love and respect each other on their wedding day get to the point of utter disgust towards one another after being married for a few years? It happens each day we fail to take advantage of the opportunity to show respect to one another. Just like we must choose to love, we must choose to respect each other as well...even on those days when we can't think of anything that our spouse has done to gain our respect. I know this is counter-cultural, but it's so important that we do this for our spouse. We need to let our spouse know that we appreciate what he/she does and most importantly, who he/she is. A simple, genuine compliment goes a long way. We can't do it too much.

3. MUTUAL SUBMISSION.

Submission gets a bad rap...even in the Christian community. God meant submission to be a good thing and to be mutual. When both the husband and wife resist being selfish and commit to serve one another, the marriage will thrive. Healthy marital submission occurs when we submit to God first and then to one another. We must humble ourselves and build trust. A marriage cannot survive without trust. In marriage, we either both win or both lose. When we mutually submit to each other, we surrender our defenses and come together as one. When we do this, we both win every time. There are certainly specific roles that God assigns to the husband and the wife. I believe our culture has made some of these roles seem oppressive for wives. This is simply untrue.

4. KINDNESS.

This should be a no-brainer, but I know too many married couples who communicate in the most unkind of ways — with words and actions — on a daily basis. This is toxic to our marriage and families and it is simply wrong. We must be mindful of our words and choose kindness every time. Let's not be kind to all of our co-workers and perfect strangers we encounter only to come home and verbally throw up on each other or ignore one another. It's not Okay. We can't assume that our spouse knows that we love him/her and that we are just venting. Words hurt and leave scars. Proverbs 12:25 says, "Anxiety weighs down the heart, but kind word cheers up the heart." Let's give our kindest words and gestures to our families and cheer them up. The world can beat us up sometimes. Our homes should be a place of peace, love, and encouragement, even when we disagree.

5. DAILY COMMUNICATION.

Again, this seems like a given and yet so many couples struggle in this area. We need to talk — with words — to one another. Put down the phone. Turn off the television. Close the laptop. We must remove distractions when it comes to effective communication with our spouse. Give him/her your eyes. I struggle with this too sometimes. God made us to crave connection and in this day and age, we are more connected than ever. However, nothing replaces face-to-face conversation. Let's give our wives our best attention, not a half-hearted glance from a device. Friends, let's put it all away and share our heart with our spouse. Dream together. Laugh together. Cry together. That daily heart-to-heart conversation is the cornerstone of true intimacy.

6. SEXUAL INTIMACY.

Sex is important. God designed it to be a beautiful culmination of love, intimacy, trust, commitment and pleasure specifically for a husband and wife. Sex is a good thing and it should never be abused. We shouldn't use it as a punishment or reward and we certainly shouldn't withhold it or force it upon one another. In fact, we will have the best sex when we mutually submit to one another's desires.

7. NON-SEXUAL PHYSICAL TOUCH.

Physical touch plays a vital role in our marriage, but it doesn't always need to lead to sex. A simple hug, pat on the back, kiss, shoulder rub, foot rub or holding of hands is an intimate gesture of reassurance for the love we feel for one another. Some couples are naturally more affectionate than others, but every couple needs to offer some non-sexual physical touch to one another. Cuddle when you watch television. Hold hands when you go on a walk. Give each other a foot rub. When we willingly serve our partner by engaging in the kind of physical touch that makes him/her feel loved, we will strengthen our marriage.

8. FOUNDATION OF FAITH.

I believe this is the most important must-have of all. Every marriage will go through rough patches. We are frail human beings who makes mistakes and are in dire need of a Savior. I thank God every day that He chose to send His Son, Jesus Christ, to be our one and only Savior. He took on all of our sins-even the nastiest, most hateful, disgusting, heart-wrenching, humanly unforgivable ones. He died and paid the price for our sins and rose again so we can live a life of freedom. His love is unfailing even when our love for one another falls short. His grace is ever-extended when we can't find it in our hearts to forgive. When both the husband and wife have a strong faith in the Lord — both individually and collectively — the foundation for the marriage is strong. They can cover their marriage and family in prayer and know the peace and love that only God can provide. If faith in Jesus is new to you, I encourage you to read the Gospels in the Bible to learn about Jesus and His tremendous love for you. Becoming a Christian doesn't mean you will be perfect, but it does mean that you will know and be known by a flawless, loving God who has perfect plans for you.

"A MESSAGE FROM GOD"

As we close the final day's reading, I want to share a story with you that forever changed our perspective about perseverance. I have never heard God audibly speak, but a few years ago, I did receive a message from God in a very unlikely way. This simple two-word message changed my life and I believe it has the power to change your life and your marriage, as well.

I had just moved my family to a new city and was serving as a pastor in a new church. The transitions and pressures of life and ministry with a young family were beginning to feel overwhelming. I felt exhausted, misunderstood, frustrated, discouraged and near the end of my rope. I wanted to quit. For the first time in my adult life, I wanted to do anything but ministry!

I was sharing all of this with my Ashley one night and finally in frustration, I stood up from the couch and began to stomp around the living room like a toddler and said, "God, it feels like you are being completely quiet right now! Where are you? I could really use a message from you. Just tell me what I'm supposed to do here!" I plopped back on the couch in frustration and threw my feet up on the coffee table. Then, Ashley said, "You've got something stuck on your foot." I looked down and there was a sticker on my heel. It must have been left on the floor by one of my kids. As I peeled it off to look at it, I had to catch my breath because I was overwhelmed by what it said. I was (and still am) convinced that sticker on my foot was as clear a message from God as I have ever received. It simply said, "KEEP GOING!"

That marked a turning point in my attitude and my perspective. I wrote the date "6-30-10" on that sticker and placed it on the front page of my Bible as a constant reminder to keep going. God gave me the strength to press through that difficult season and very quickly, almost every area of life and ministry began to improve.

We've all had moments where we've felt like giving up and moments where we've wondered where God is in all of it. I pray that you are reminded that God is with you, He is for you, He will carry you through the struggle, He will bring purpose from your pain and He will reward your faithfulness. Just don't give up. Keep going until you reach the finish line!

In your marriage, you will face great times and tough times, but if you'll hold onto God, hold onto each other and commit to simply keep going, there is nothing that can stop you or tear you apart!

"...And let us run with endurance the race God has set before us. We do this by keeping our eyes on Jesus, the champion who initiates and perfects our faith." *Hebrews 12:1-2*

LIVING THE SEVENTH PROMISE:

"I WILL LOVE YOU 'TIL DEATH DO US PART."

Remember that a "perfect marriage" is just two imperfect people who refuse to give up on each other! In every season of your life together, make each other a priority. Be intentional of about developing the healthy habits that will set a positive course for your marriage. Keep loving each other, keep encouraging each other, keep praying together and keep going until God calls you home. Now, get ready to today's activity because the entire experience has been building up to this moment!

DAY
SEVEN
—
Activity

When was the last time you wrote a "love letter" to your spouse? When Ashley and I lead marriage retreats and events, one exercise we always include involves each husband and wife writing a love letter to each other. When we explain the exercise, some people roll their eyes as if their inner dialogue is saying, "This is so cheesy! I haven't written a love letter since middle school."

We assure them that they need to trust us and this exercise will be well worth the effort. We remind them that our words have such power and when we use our words to encourage and adore our spouses, our words can instantly improve intimacy in our marriages. We instruct them to not just say, "I love you," but to write specific attributes they love about each other. We encourage them to share their feelings as honestly and specifically as they can.

Near the end of our time together, we have the couples each go to a place on the property where they can have some privacy and then take turns reading the letters to each other. At the end of their time of sharing, we encourage them to hold hands and pray together. During the prayer, we suggest that they should thank God for each other, pray about their dreams and hopes for the marriage, confess any negative behavior they need to change and recommit their lives to God and to each other.

After the love letter exercise is complete, the couples return to the group and share. Many of the couples who had rolled their eyes before the exercise had tears in their eyes. We've had numerous couples tell us that the exercise was one of the most significant milestones in their marriage and the love letter from their spouse would be one of their most treasured possessions on earth.

Each time we lead couples through this time of sharing and see the impact their words can make on one another, we're reminded that words can shape a marriage. Your words, spoken with thoughtfulness, tenderness and love have immense power. Use your words to build your spouse up, not to tear him or her down. Use your words to be your spouse's biggest encourager; not his or her biggest critic. In every interaction with your spouse, live out the command of *Ephesians 4:29* which says, "Do not let any unwholesome talk come out of your mouths, but only what is helpful for building others up according to their needs, that it may benefit those who listen."

CREATING A MILE-STONE MOMENT IN YOUR MARRIAGE

___

In this final chapter, we want to give you the opportunity to experience a milestone moment with your wife. It's going to require some thought and preparation on your part, but we promise, it will be well worth the effort! We'll begin with the love letter exercise and then move into a time of renewing your vows and then making a renewed promise of re-commitment to each other.

The first step is to take time to write a letter to each other. You can type and print it out if necessary, but I encourage you write the letter in your own handwriting. We've found that handwritten letters have become so rare in our culture, that when we do receive them (especially from a spouse), they are more likely to become a keepsake. We believe your wife will treasure your letter for years to come! Once you've both written the letter, choose a time and place to sit down and take turns reading them. While your wife is reading, let them finish before you respond to their words. End the exercise by sharing your thoughts and feelings with each other and then transitioning into the renewing of your vows.

This would also be an ideal time to say a prayer with each other and for each other. Hold hands and take turns praying aloud thanking God for your marriage and asking His blessings and guidance for the next season of your journey.

RENEW
-ING
THE
VOWS

Now that you've made it to the end of this journey to the vows and you hopefully have a renewed understanding of the six promises that will make or break a marriage, let's take a moment to recap each one. I'd encourage you to repeat these words to each other as a way to recommit your lives to each other and begin a new season of growth in your marriage.

Before you exchange these words, let start with a quick recap of what each of these vows really means:

1. "I TAKE YOU TO BE MY HUSBAND/WIFE."

In the entire world, you could only give this gift of your love to one person. You have chosen your spouse and they have chosen you! Never lose sight of this beautiful exchange. Be the best husband or wife you can be for them.

2. "TO LOVE AND TO CHERISH."

God calls husbands and wives to adore each other and to pursue each other with an ever-growing love. This is a commitment to invest in the friendship that sets the foundation for romantic love. It means to be creatively, thoughtfully and passionately working to win the heart of your spouse over and over again.

3. "FOR BETTER OR FOR WORSE."

You've got to love each other no matter what. Marital love can't be based on convenience or even feelings. This commitment means that our love will never be based on our circumstances. Your vows are most important in the moments when they are least convenient.

4. "IN SICKNESS OR IN HEALTH."

You can't always control what happens to your health, but you can also control how you choose to respond. Recommit to loving and supporting each other completely in moments of health, but also in moments of injury or illness.

5. "FORSAKING ALL OTHERS."

Marriage must remain monogamous. Refuse to allow anyone else to steal your spouse's rightful place in your mind, your heart or your bed. Recommit to loving each other with wholehearted fidelity and devotion.

6. "FOR RICHER OR FOR POORER."

Commit to each other that money will never be your primary pursuit. Your love has nothing to do with whether you're bankrupt or wealthy. Money comes and money goes, but your commitment to each other must stand firm.

7. "UNTIL DEATH DO US PART."

Remember that these vows you are renewing are made with no expiration clause and no exit strategy. You're in this for life and you wouldn't want it any other way!

Once you've had a moment to reflect upon the significance of the vows and the journey you've taken up to this point, please take your spouse's hand and repeat these sacred promises to each other:

"I _____ ,

take you _____ ,

To love and to cherish, for better or for worse, for richer or for poorer, in sickness or in health, forsaking all others, 'til death do us part!"

You may now kiss the bride!

Congratulations! You've come to the end of this journey, but it's really much more of a starting point than a finish line. We hope this course has helped you refuel your relationship and refocus your resolve as you look to the road ahead. I pray God's continued blessings and guidance for you both through all the celebrations and challenges of life. If you'll continue to walk through life hand-in-hand, trusting God and supporting each other, there's nothing that can come between you!

What did I learn about my spouse today?

What did I learn about my myself today?

As a result of what I'm learning, I'm committing to take the following actions to strengthen my marriage-

_____

_____

_____

_____

_____

_____

_____

_____

_____

_____

_____

_____

_____

_____

_____

_____

_____

_____

Today, my prayer for my marriage is-

_____

_____

_____

_____

_____

_____

_____

_____

_____

_____

_____

_____

_____

_____

_____

_____

_____

ACKNOWLEDGEMENTS

First off, we want to thank you for reading this book and making this investment into your marriage. We hope this resource has helped you. We're honored that you've trusted us to be a small part of your journey and we are praying God's continued blessings for your marriage in the days ahead!

Our heartfelt thanks go out to the entire team at StrongerMarriages.com for their continued partnership in creating resources to build stronger marriages and families. We also want to thank our online readers for shaping much of the content in this book through sharing their stories, struggles and insights with us. Finally, we are deeply indebted to our many friends, mentors and associates who have prayed for us, encouraged us, taught us and cheered us on. We're truly blessed to be surrounded by such a loving and supportive community.

With much love and gratitude,
Dave and Ashley Willis

Season one traces the almost failed marriage of the hosts, Melanie and Seth Studley, and explores parallel stories of other marriages with similar struggles.

Download or subscribe at www.strongermarriagespodcast.com or www.anatomyofmarriage.com

MORE THAN A BOOK

Going through 31 Creative Ways To Love And Encourage Him & Her with your significant other will:

- Bring more joy to your relationship.

- Give you tools and practical ways to serve him or her.

- Spark love, fun, and adventure back into the relationship.

- Teach you about one another.

- Create lasting memories.

- Help you develop the language to grow in healthy communication.

Get 3 free videos from us

free.fightingformymarriage.com

The first steps to healing a wounded marriage

How to instantly improve communication

The keys to rekindling intimacy

If you enjoyed

"7 Days to a Stronger Marriage,"

check out the bestselling book
by Dave Willis,

THE
SEVEN
LAWS
OF LOVE

to learn the timeless principles that can
help you build stronger relationships
with everyone in your life.

www.7LawsOfLoveBook.com

FOREWORD BY **SHAUNTI FELDHAHN**
NEW YORK TIMES BESTSELLING AUTHOR OF
FOR WOMEN ONLY AND *FOR MEN ONLY*

THE SEVEN LAWS OF L⊙VE

ESSENTIAL PRINCIPLES FOR
BUILDING STRONGER RELATIONSHIPS

DAVE WILLIS